AF470551

Against the World
Playing for England

Kevin Keegan

with
Mike Langley

Sidgwick & Jackson
London

First published in Great Britain in 1979
by Sidgwick and Jackson Limited

Copyright © 1979 by Kevin Keegan, Mike Langley and
Sidgwick and Jackson Limited

Designed by Paul Turner

Picture research by Anne Horton

Author's acknowledgements
Particular thanks for guidance, assistance or
contributions to this book are due to Stan Cullis,
Reg Drury, Norman Fox, Glen Kirton, Robert
Schrecker, Bill Taylor, George Antonio
Rowlands and Mrs Daphne Blanch.

ISBN 0 283 98539 9 (hard)
ISBN 0 283 98540 2 (paper)

Phototypeset by Oliver Burridge & Co. Ltd, Crawley
Printed in Great Britain by
The Garden City Press Limited
Letchworth, Hertfordshire
SG6 1JS
for Sidgwick and Jackson Limited
1 Tavistock Chambers, Bloomsbury Way
London WC1A 2SG

Contents

Foreword 7

1　First Appearances 9

2　The Decline of England 17

3　Home Internationals 25

4　Against the World 33

5　Managers 43

6　On Tour with Revie 51

7　The Team Behind the Team 65

8　Keepers 77

Colour section 81

9　Players 97

10　Supporters 107

11　Germany 113

12　The Greatest – My Own Selection 123

13　Off the Pitch 133

14　To the Summit 137

My Games for England 141

England Matches Since 1966 143

Index 159

Photo Acknowledgements 160

Foreword

Petrol was rationed and the foreign currency allowance was £25, a pittance even in those days, when I set off with a friend in his old, side-valve Morris Minor for my first England tour.

It was 1952. The Red Army still occupied parts of Austria, and Russian tommy-gunners ringed the Prater Stadium as Nat Lofthouse's long, solo run for the winning goal immortalized him as 'The Lion of Vienna'. Zurich and Florence were the other venues. England drew with the Italians and beat the Swiss, so our final, straitened days of sleeping in fields and living on bread and salami seemed a small price for the glory of an undefeated tour.

Football writers have a word, less disparaging than it may sound, for fans whose allegiances are indulged beyond the normal. Such fans are known as punters, and their numbers include those Scots who hitch-hiked through the Andes to Argentina last summer as well as the Englishman who abandoned a fortnight's holiday after seeing only one match in the Mexico World Cup. He flew in, England lost, and he flew straight out again. Twenty-seven years ago, before package tours and credit cards and drive-on ferries, I was an England punter, and perhaps I still am, although the magnificent philanthropy of newspaper proprietors transports me in the team's plane and opens the doors of hotels fit for presidents.

I first met Kevin Keegan on an England flight; we argued about cricket. Our journeys since have ranged from the Danube to Disneyland. I remember, particularly, lunch on a golf course in Argentina, and how, but for his superb reflexes at the wheel, we would have piled up on sheet ice this year down a German lane. The serious work on this book has been done in Copenhagen, Dublin, London, Hamburg and Sofia.

My part in this joint enterprise was to compile the statistics, mark out the pitch, hold the watch, take a few throw-ins and do the typing as Kevin's natural vitality and inside knowledge crackled into the tape recorder. He doesn't drink and I wouldn't; we got high together on optimism, on our belief in a regenerated England. We disagreed on next to nothing as my original vague idea took shape as his book, and the opinions in it are undiluted Keegan.

Mike Langley
June 1979

1 First Appearances

I have set myself certain targets – targets to do with fitness, scoring and skill, financial targets. More of them have been fulfilled than I would once have thought possible – except with England, the team that means everything to me.

Two World Cups passing us by is the biggest scandal in sport, yet it is not only the players and the managers who are to blame. Everyone in the administration of English football is partly responsible. Somewhere at the top we went wrong, and these questions still remain unanswered: was our planning right? is Wembley the right ground for us? has there been too much red tape?

I was on the bench behind Sir Alf Ramsey on 17 October 1973 when our draw with Poland at Wembley stopped us from qualifying for the 1974 World Cup in West Germany. Goalkeeper Jan Tomaszewski – 'A clown', as Brian Clough so mistakenly called him – was stopping everything. Then, with perhaps five minutes left, Sir Alf turned his head and said, 'Kevin, get changed!' I shot to my feet, and Ray Clemence beside me was so excited that, in trying to help take off my tracksuit, he whipped my shorts and under-pants down to my knees. And then I found that Alf had meant the other forward substitute, Kevin Hector of Derby County, who darted on for probably the briefest of England debuts, something like ninety seconds. It was agony having to sit and watch as the score stayed stuck at 1–1. Not for a whole day did it sink

in that England had failed to qualify for the first time, and that the world was going to Munich without us.

Three years later, in Rome, I captained England in our 0–2 World Cup defeat by Italy, the result that started our skid out of the race to qualify for Argentina. Since that day I have never moved out of a wall. Italy's first goal was a free kick that deflected off me because I was thinking, having blocked a similar shot by bursting out minutes earlier, 'If it's right once, it's right twice.' But when I flew out this time the ball cannoned off me and whistled past Ray Clemence.

Now my target is Spain in 1982 and, being realistic, that is my last World Cup chance. I'll be thirty-one then, still young enough to be an asset to the squad but old enough to be aware of the growing threat to my position from the likes of Trevor Francis, Tony Woodcock, Laurie Cunningham and Cyrille Regis. I accept their challenge, and can say that every lad coming into the present England squad is made welcome; I think that is why newcomers are finding their feet more quickly. There is no bitchiness and hardly any of the resentful 'Oh, this kid has pushed my mate out', or the fearful 'Oh, he's after my place.'

For myself, I trust in versatility. I could adjust to another position because I will never abandon my last and greatest target, playing with England in the finals of a World Cup. When I signed for Hamburg the most important factor for me was not the money, not what the Germans might achieve with me, nor what Liverpool would do without me.

All smiles from Jan Tomaszewski and a Polish fan after the famous 1–1 draw at Wembley

No, the vital thing was the clause guaranteeing my release for England games. It's a wonderful feeling to play for England; more marvellous still is captaining England and leading out the best eleven footballers in the country. When the anthem starts, I love to sing it.

I first led out England in a setting that was anything but glamorous, a wet, muddy Wednesday night at Wrexham. The appointment surprised everyone, not least myself, for only ten months earlier I had walked out on manager Don Revie. But Revie, always a man for detail, felt this particular team required a northern captain; also he knew that I lived only eighteen miles from the ground. So he made me captain, and I retained this honour for eleven matches.

Then Ron Greenwood removed it from me, giving as his reasons that I didn't earn my living in England any more, and that I was a forward, a bad position for captains. 'Don't take it personally,' he said, 'but I'm giving the job to Emlyn Hughes.'

Although I saw his reasons, I couldn't pretend not to be disappointed. Once a captain it is natural to want the job permanently and, without contradicting Ron Greenwood, the most important thing about a captain is not the number on his shirt but the amount of respect the other players have for him. As was seen in the last World Cup with Dino Zoff of Italy, even goalkeepers can skipper international sides if their reputation stands high enough with their team-mates. The captain ought also to be your best-known player because that frightens the

A study in dejection – Don Revie (left) in Rome watching us lose 2–0 to Italy in a World Cup qualifier, November 1976

opposition. When Johan Cruyff walked out first for Holland, you could see the other team thinking, 'He looks like a god, and he's the captain!' Believe me, many battles are won before the kick-off.

It seems odd in a way to be mourning the captaincy when, for a long time, I struggled just to establish myself as an England player. My first target was simply to become a regular international, someone whose name appeared on the team-sheet without anyone complaining, 'Didn't do very well last time, did he?' or 'How about a chance for a younger lad?' I played almost twenty matches for England before finding my feet. I had never imagined it would take so long.

The first call came without any ceremony. An international cap is the dream of many small boys and the summit of many an adult career, yet it is never heralded by a knock from the telegram boy or an engraved invitation pushed through the letter box. The Football Association send out individual letters, but they always arrive after the team has been announced in the newspapers and on the radio. Sometimes at Hamburg I have not received the letter of selection until after playing in the match.

We still get the traditional England caps, though, styled in rich blue velvet with silver quartering and a tassel. I took one to the *Volkspark* and made my German team-mates quite envious; they are paid nearly four times as much as English players for international appearances, but money goes, whereas a cap lasts and can be an heirloom. I learned of my first cap from a friend who heard a radio bulletin and phoned me. I could hardly believe it, and felt that I had been pushed in by the media as the kid from Scunthorpe who just happened to have made a flying start at Liverpool.

It was a bad time to join England. The team was in transition and under a manager who may not have been convinced that I was ready for a full cap but was willing to take a gamble. Sir Alf Ramsey probably regarded me at that stage as ready for the squad rather than for the team.

He knew me because of a tour of Under-23 matches in East Germany, Poland and Russia in the summer of 1972. I had been sent off for retaliating against an East German who dealt out terrible stick off the ball. Sir Alf not only supported me in a letter to the Football Association but picked me for the other two matches. No experience could have been more valuable. It's in grim Iron Curtain cities that character is proved, not at Wembley with 100,000 supporters chanting 'England'. When someone tells me a star is born, I am always inclined to say, 'Well, let's test him in Bulgaria. Or Russia.' That tour was a spine-stiffening introduction to international football, but it still left me unprepared for the big-time of a World Cup qualifying match in Wales.

I cannot say there was unfriendliness from the established players in the senior squad, yet I was aware of cliques and felt like an intruder. The unspoken attitude was: 'Here's a newcomer, a young kid who has had a lot of press exposure. Let's see him prove it.' Years later Alan Ball said to me about that debut in Cardiff, 'You were scared stiff.' I am not a nervous player so what Ball probably meant, which was true, was that I was somewhat overawed. Only fifteen months earlier I had been in the Third Division with Scunthorpe and suddenly I was in the England team alongside stars I had watched as a schoolboy.

Ball himself was my hero in the 1966 World Cup. I spent three weeks glued to the television admiring this little red-head running round for England when clubs were telling me, 'You're too small, too puny to be a pro.' He was everything that I believed I was: he had the same build, he ran a lot, he had

A trio of immortals. Left to right: Sir Alf Ramsey, Bobby Charlton and Sir Matt Busby

loads of skill and plenty of vision. Probably I am a shade stronger than Ball, but basically that was me on the screen. Naturally, I was over-awed at playing with him for the first time; everyone is over-awed on their England debut, although they pretend they are not.

The team game of football is really an individual matter for a new international player. First, he must prove his right to a place. Thoughts of the overall team performance come a long way second to that. I sat in the dressing room at Ninian Park, Cardiff, on 15 November 1972, reading and re-reading a pile of telegrams and remembering as much as I could of Sir Alf's pre-match instructions which, in a nutshell, were: 'Go out and enjoy it. Play as you do for Liverpool.' The snag about such apparently straightforward advice was the assumption that the other England forwards would adopt the same roles as my team-mates at Anfield.

Martin Chivers, the best England centre forward of that time, didn't play at all like John Toshack of Liverpool, as I soon found out. Nor could I discover where Rodney Marsh fitted into the attack, for he never said much to anybody; I knew he was deaf in one ear and had heard it said, 'He's deaf in the other when he wants to be.' Chivers was a big man, able to take defenders away from me; Marsh had plenty of skill. I thought the formation might work if I could operate between them, but when I ran nobody moved out of the way. It was not like Liverpool at all.

Then came the incident that made me realize what a long road lay ahead before I could consider myself an England player; it began when I broke clear of the Welsh defence and had only to beat the goalkeeper, Gary Sprake. I jinked right, I jinked left, but he refused to move. He stood still, watching my approach to about seven yards from goal. The only gap showing was between his legs, so I tried something that is not in my normal repertoire. I tried a nutmeg, which is what we call that show-off ball drilled through an opponent's legs. Of course, he saved it. He got a knee to the ball, or the ball hit his knee, and I had missed a goal. I had frozen. Sprake had psyched me out of it. He made me do the thinking, and that was the early warning that playing for England was not going to be easy. I didn't get a good press but Alf said, 'Don't worry what the papers say, I'm sticking by you.'

So I was in for the next game, in January 1973, against Wales again and again a World Cup qualifier; this was also my Wembley debut. I looked forward to it, imagining wide-open spaces, slaughtered Welsh lambs and a guaranteed home win. Yes, I had some Roy of the Rovers ideas in those days when, only twenty-one, I was being pushed commercially and in football as the brightest new star since George Best. I felt a duty to live up to my publicity; instead, I again froze round the box. Indeed, we all did, and were booed off for drawing 1–1 after having something like 80 per cent of the play. Nothing went for me, nothing I tried. I went off absolutely drained by tension and by the effort of working twice as hard as I did for Liverpool.

Then, a few months later, in my third appearance for England – and, curiously, once more against Wales – I scored. Not a splendid goal, just a tap-in, but pleasing nonetheless. I hadn't played well but that goal got me going, started me feeling that perhaps I belonged in the team. I sensed, too, that the other lads were helping more as they realized my problems of adjustment.

A professional footballer always seeks psychological props during a bad spell. If you are knocking in goals, you tell yourself, 'Maybe I'm not playing well, but I am scoring.' If you are missing chances, you say, 'At least I'm making goals for the others.' And if you are doing neither then the consoling thought might be, 'I'm only playing badly because of injury.' What kept me going through the hard early years with England was the knowledge that although I hadn't played well at least we had never lost. I had sixteen caps before playing on a losing side – not sixteen consecutively because I was in and out, but the sequence of results provided my little reassurance, my excuse for telling myself I wasn't that bad.

On the field I found inspiration in Colin Bell, who had suffered the same difficulty in adapting to international football. If you judged him on his first ten matches, you could forget him as an England player. I came into the team in the era of Bell. He was the man, the number one England footballer, and great to play with. Roy McFarland and Colin Todd were good, but Bell ran the show.

His work-rate was incredible; I remember a goal against Czechoslovakia in October 1974 when he started in our penalty area and ran the length of

Wembley to slot in the ball. Only Bell could have scored that. Nijinsky, we called him – after the racehorse, not the ballet dancer. I would not have liked to compete with him in anything at that time; he was so fit. Yet he always looked ill, a ghastly, anaemic white. As a man, he was very quiet and sincere, and I believe the loss of Colin Bell through a knee injury was the reason for England first going downhill after the great start under Don Revie. It was even more devastating than the loss as a result of serious back injury, only eight months later, of Gerry Francis.

The most powerful influence on my career, though, was not a player, but a manager. I owe my England caps to Bill Shankly of Scotland. He signed me for Liverpool, opened my eyes, made me a player; he was the first to instil into me the idea of targets. 'Jesus Christ,' he was always saying, 'you're a great player. You're not just a great player, you're one of THE great players.'

Shankly gave me something to prove; I started becoming a good player because he swore that I was one. When others joined the chorus, I found something within my armoury that helped me do justice to their assessments. I can motivate myself now, but as a fresh kid from a small club I needed someone to believe in me. Shankly was the man; if I had gone to another manager I probably wouldn't be where I am today. Shankly pushed me mercilessly and convinced me that there was little to fear even against famous internationals. I caused problems for Big Jack Charlton and Bobby Moore and

I've included this picture as a reminder to forwards that they shouldn't try to be too clever. It's the incident when Gary Sprake of Wales psyched me out of a goal at Cardiff in 1972

The fans, the Cup, the man. It's Bill Shankly with the championship trophy after Liverpool won the League in 1973. Tommy Smith is on the left

began telling myself, 'Hell, I'm almost as good as they are, and they're coming down while I'm going up.'

I'll never forget my first game against Moore, captain of West Ham and of the England team that won the World Cup. I had been a Liverpool player for barely four months, and it was the same year that Bobby and three other Hammers had been shopped for visiting a Blackpool nightclub on the eve of an F.A. Cup tie.

Shankly always stood in the dressing room passage to inspect the opposition. Nothing escaped him. He noted how they dressed, if they had shaved, how their hair was cut, if they looked out of sorts, if their gait betrayed any trace of injury. He studied the Hammers' arrival and then, beckoning me to a corner of the dressing room, said, 'Jesus Christ, son. I've just seen that Bobby Moore. Big bags under his eyes. Limping. He's been out in a nightclub last night again, son. You can tell.' His gaze darted round the rest of the team, then his voice – of defiant, undiminished Scottishness despite a lifetime in England – barked unforgettably, 'He's scared stiff of playing against you, son. You'll run him silly.'

I ran out of the tunnel really believing that my

'Mr Perfect' himself – Bobby Moore – cutting out an Arsenal attack at West Ham, December 1971. And that's Ray Kennedy before transferring from Highbury to Anfield

opponent was among the poorest players ever seen in the Football League – and I scored, and we won 3-1, and I played well. But Moore was magnificent. When I returned to the dressing room afterwards, Shankly sat beside me again and said, 'Jesus Christ, son. What a great player that Bobby Moore is. You'll never play against a better player than him.' Shankly, that marvellous motivator, knew the necessity of not belittling someone against whom I had played well.

I have talked with Shankly for hours; it was a privilege to know him and to watch how he went about instilling heart and hope into teams and players. When I was having my early bad time with England, he kept saying, 'They don't know how to play you. They don't know where your position is. Don't they ever come and watch you play for Liverpool to see what you can do? Don't they know how to get the best out of you?' Suddenly it was England's fault, not my fault. Exposure to the Shankly stimulant cures all depressions; you think 'Perhaps he's right', and you pick yourself up and keep going.

But, as I was to discover over the next few years, the troubles of England were too deep-rooted for a merely verbal remedy.

LIVERPOOL ARE MAGIC
LIVERPOOL F.C.
LIVERPOOL
SUPER LIVERPOOL

2 The Decline of England

I danced in a Doncaster pub-disco one summer evening nine years ago neither knowing nor caring that, thousands of miles away, Bobby Charlton's champagne had gone flat.

It was 14 June 1970, the gloomy Sunday when we lost to the West Germans in Mexico, the last time that England played in the finals of a World Cup. I didn't bother to watch the whole two hours' play on the pub T.V. When Uwe Seeler's back-header looped over Peter Bonetti – a really clever equalizer – I remember standing up and saying to a girl with me, 'They've had it, they've gone.' I just knew that England were dead, perhaps crushed by ninety degrees of noonday sun as much as anything else. Yet the inquest into our defeat rumbles on, never returning a unanimous verdict, and the story of Charlton's funereal party has passed into the team legends. I have heard it so often that the scene is in my head like a clip from an old film.

Sometimes it seems I was there, beside the motel swimming pool in dusty Leon, just across the road from the ground where Germany, although 2–0 down with only twenty minutes left, sent us into extra time and defeat in this quarter-final. White-jacketed waiters are hurrying about with trays of champagne ordered and chilled since morning to celebrate Bobby Charlton's record 106th cap. No one had imagined then that the real toast would be to the finale of his international career. Sir Alf Ramsey is stunned and alone in his cabin, although

persuaded out later. Alan Ball, in a rage, hurls his World Cup winner's medal through an open window. Gordon Banks, who had been struck off the team list by Montezuma's Revenge, is still pale and weak from an afternoon spent darting between bed and lavatory. The only relief to the misery of Banks had been a mistaken belief that England had finished a goal ahead. Now he knows the truth. Bonetti, Banks' replacement, is already flying with his wife for a holiday in Acapulco, unaware of the witch-hunt back home where everyone blames him for diving over a shot from Franz Beckenbauer to give Germany their first goal.

People also blamed Sir Alf Ramsey for taking off Bobby Charlton and Martin Peters and sending on Norman Hunter and Colin Bell as substitutes. The whole of England argued for weeks but I sat out the debate, being at that time more interested in girls than in international football. When I thought about it later, and knew more of the facts, it seemed that Sir Alf had made his substitutions because of the 400-mile coach ride next day to Mexico City, where there would be only one full day's rest before facing Italy in the semi-final at an extra 2,000 feet of altitude. Naturally, he wanted to save players' legs, and, ninety-nine times out of a hundred, this would have been a smart tactical move. Instead, it backfired. What I never foresaw were the long repercussions of that defeat, nor how, after kicking off that Sunday as World Cup-holders, at least a dozen years would drag by before England could again figure in the tournament proper.

There is no single reason for our failure to qualify

'You'll never walk alone' is the song, and here's a typical picture proving it

for the 1974 and 1978 World Cups. It wasn't simply that Sir Alf became stereotyped or that Don Revie turned indecisive. A whole combination of factors are to blame; one of them is Wembley itself. We play our home matches on a foreign ground. Nowhere else in England is there a ground ringed by a track and with the crowd miles away. But almost every major German club has that layout, as do most other Continental clubs. Continentals march from our tunnel to find themselves more at home than we are.

Footballers in England grow up with the crowd on top of them, with stands and terraces hemming them in. They are used to compactness, so Wembley seems huge, even though several First Division pitches – not to mention little Doncaster – are wider and longer. And the problem of adjustment to Wembley is not only the lack of atmosphere but, because of the openness, a loss of the familiar markers by which we judge passing distances in club games.

I think England also spent too long in the early seventies seeking a new Nobby Stiles, toothless terror of the 1966 team. Nobby is a wonderful wee man, rightly one of football's most popular characters – but no one seemed to notice that his type of ferocious ball-winning was undergoing some sophisticated development on the Continent, particularly in Germany and Italy. They saw the need for a ball-winning marker as used by England, but decided that the job should be done by a dual-purpose player with the skill to move up as an inside forward as well as the concentration and power to shadow and tackle. Bonhof of Germany and Tardelli of Italy immediately spring to mind as fulfilling that role, while the outstanding example is Benetti of Italy, who can be as delicate in placing a pass as he is mighty in winning the ball. With that kind of all-rounder in midfield, the Continentals had twelve men to our eleven.

England's eventual replacement for Stiles was Peter Storey, who once revealed his attitude and limitations by saying, 'If it wasn't for people like me, the Sugar Plum Fairy could play centre forward.' Storey played some fine games but, on

Trevor Brooking (right) at Wembley on the night we beat Italy 2–0 with the help of one of his rare international goals, November 1977

19

balance, was lucky to collect eighteen international caps. I look on that era as a turn down the wrong road.

Hard-man football, as typified by Storey, made us unpopular. An acid comment from Gunter Netzer, later to become my boss at Hamburg, went round the world after a violent goalless draw in West Berlin. 'The whole English team have autographed my right leg,' said Netzer. Only a fortnight later a bad-tempered England victory at Hampden Park was condemned by Hugh Nelson, president of the Scottish F.A., who said, 'If this is international football, it's a disgrace.'

The hard men were swept from the squad by Joe Mercer, the caretaker manager for seven matches after the sacking of Sir Alf in April 1974. It was an important contribution; for the first time, I felt we had an England team able to play from the back to the front. Joe picked entertaining players, the kind that fans might have selected. I was particularly pleased by the choice of Alec Lindsay, the left back who made me tick at Liverpool and who joked, with justification, 'I've thumped so many passes to your chest, there's "Mitre" stamped on it.'

But the bubbly nature of Mercer's squad was lost within a year after a beginning of rich promise under Don Revie when we slaughtered Czechoslovakia, who later won the European championship, and when we gave the West Germans their first defeat as World Cup-holders. Decline set in, partly because of injuries to Colin Bell and skipper Gerry Francis but mainly because of a levelling out

Not so much a crowd as a stimulant – that's the Kop.

of talent. It became possible to pick five useful England teams but not a single great side.

One factor in this was that too many brilliant youngsters failed to fulfil their potential and our expectations. Dave Thomas, a winger in the first Revie team, is just such a case. Thomas was playing world-class football with Burnley in the First Division while I was stuck in the backwoods with Scunthorpe. In those days I believed he had a tremendous international future, but time has shown that he cannot quite bridge the gap separating the club player from the international.

So many likely lads never make that step up – Steve Perryman of Tottenham, for instance. He reached such a high standard as a teenager that everyone assumed he would keep on improving, a common mistake in assessing bright youngsters. I made it myself in Perryman's case. We played together in England's Under-23 team and I would have put money on him to succeed at the top level. He was a 100 per center with everything except real pace, but lack of speed never caused him to be exposed. He compensated with a big heart and a gigantic appetite for work; nobody ran past Steve Perryman. Yet he didn't make it as a full international.

It is hard to be sure if the fault is in the players' personalities or with their clubs. For example, Martin Dobson was always being tipped as an automatic England player at Burnley, where he won the first of his few caps, but he went backwards on joining Everton, perhaps unable to adjust after being the big fish in a little pond.

Another disappointment was Peter Taylor, who came on as substitute when I captained England for the first time. He was a winger from Crystal Palace and the first Third Division player to be capped since Johnny Byrne, also of the Palace, in 1961. Taylor looked very good that night; I thought he was going to be a real asset to the team. He was skilful, positive and quick. Yet, although Tottenham were impressed enough to pay £200,000 for him, Taylor the England player vanished as rapidly as he had arrived. That often happens with the overnight success.

Another growing worry was Don Revie's tendency to build a characterless squad. Lawrie McMenemy, that huge, cheerful Geordie who manages Southampton, has declared the perfect balance for a football team to be 'seven road-sweepers and four violinists'. A similar mix is needed off the field, for a team is a mechanism as intricate as a watch; all sorts of characters are needed to make it tick. You need a gambler and someone who is the soul of caution. A girl-puller must be balanced by one of nature's monks. You need a clown, and he needs team mates prepared to be the audience. You need card schools, and a few fellows who prefer paperbacks. Drinkers should be offset by teetotallers, the nightclubbers by loving husbands who go straight home.

Revie – and I will deal with him in detail later – was obviously aware of the need for mixing characters and for building the right spirit. That was the idea behind the bingo and putting sessions. He

Joe Mercer, football's jolly uncle, on the day he took over as England's caretaker-manager in 1974. It was a treat to play for him

wanted the lads together, but he didn't get full co-operation from them. Some of them didn't want bingo or putting; they putted to lose.

These problems were not helped by his reluctance to recognize that one baddie is essential in a team of goodies. Revie phased out the baddies. He selected squads of model professionals, all of them clean-living, non-clubbing, nicely-spoken, genuine chaps who would never say boo to a boss. Sometimes Revie seemed more concerned about the players' behaviour in hotels – about how neatly they dressed, how punctually they came down for breakfast, how tidily their hair was brushed – than about the performances those players were producing on Saturdays.

When I joined there was an England card school and the only disappearing artist in the squad was Martin Chivers. He would report, nod to the card-players, then go to his room. After a year or so under Revie almost the whole squad was behaving like Chivers. We had a team of invisible men. I saw most of them only for meals, training and those evening sessions of putting on the hotel carpet. There were hardly any laughs.

When I say 'baddie', I mean the unconventional player, the player who is a bit of a rebel at times. Alan Hudson, for instance. Hudson was not a work-rate footballer, nor did he conduct his life in a way that Revie might have approved. But where do you judge a player? I judge him on the field. I don't

Please note that's only a soft drink! Alan Hudson celebrates his call-up for the full England squad in 1972

It's the World Cup in Mexico, and Alan Ball has just hit Czechoslovakia's crossbar. I'll leave you to guess what he's saying!

care if a player drinks more than the average, or if he wears his hair long, or if he prefers a tee-shirt to a collar and tie. There are times when the individualist has to fall into line with the team but, in the main, as long as a player does his stuff on the field a manager should never hum and haw. I think Alan Hudson did perform for England; he added a definite touch of quality to the side. But Revie got rid of him.

An even worse mistake was getting rid of Alan Ball, a motivating captain, a great brain, and an asset even though past his best. Ball made runs, chipped passes, knocked in early balls; he was never less than totally involved and is one of the greatest England players of my time. Revie ought to have said 'Look, Bally. You are not getting through the same work and your playing area is growing smaller [which it was, as it will for me and for every other player]. But I'm keeping you in the squad.' I'm a fan of Ball only as a player, for there are aspects of his personality that don't appeal to me, yet there is no denying that he is a character, and once he had gone England began recruiting a rather characterless team. Not unexpectedly, they returned some nondescript results.

3 Home Internationals

Joey Jones was the left back at Liverpool, a club-mate and a friend. Yet he chopped me down in a Wales v. England match painfully enough to earn a rebuke from manager Bob Paisley. 'Just remember you have to play with Kevin on Saturday,' said Paisley. But that is exactly what almost no one remembers in the annual home international series between England, Scotland, Northern Ireland and Wales.

I held no grievance against Joey. The ball was between us. It was him or me, and as he was playing for Wales all Englishmen were enemies to be stopped. Fouled, if necessary. About some of the matches in this British championship it would be possible to write, 'Fouled, even when unnecessary.'

There are no private peace treaties when club-mates oppose each other, rather the reverse. The series can be disfigured by flare-ups between friends who have shared the same bathwater since schooldays. The mockery and kidding that awaits the losers on returning to their clubs is largely responsible for this. As a result identities and personal loyalties are forgotten in the battle. Regrets come later – or, as in the case of Joey Jones, sometimes instantaneously. When he realized that I was the groaning foe lying crumpled by the corner flag he got rid of the ball and ran to pick me up, almost babbling, 'Oh, I am sorry, Kevin. I never intended to do that.'

Welsh defenders never stand on ceremony, and the one who has closed up on me is among the hardest ever – John Roberts, seen here in 1974

Plenty of teeth have been spat out and even a few legs broken since the home internationals started in 1883, but I don't suppose anyone has suffered from a more evil foul than the renowned England captain and centre half Stan Cullis in a wartime match against Scotland. He was gripped by the testicles when forming a wall so savagely that he fainted, regaining consciousness to find his shorts stained with blood.

Cullis is retired from football now, his reputation unchallengeably secure as manager and creator of the long-passing Wolves when they won three League championships and two F.A. Cups with teams best remembered for Billy Wright, Bert Williams and the wingers Johnny Hancocks and Jimmy Mullen. That foul was a lifetime ago but Cullis remembers it like yesterday – as who wouldn't? He recalls: 'We were in a wall, this Scotsman stood in front of me and grabbed. I passed out. There were two sequels. He never played international football again because the English F.A. protested to the Scots, and I had to play in a support for quite a while.'

My first four games for England were against home countries, three against Wales and the fourth against Northern Ireland. They are the worst matches for introducing youngsters, for although the championship is sanctified as the oldest international series in the world I don't rate any of the fixtures as top-class. How can they be truly international when the teams consist of the same old faces who meet every Saturday in the League? There is no international atmosphere, the standard

The flying bodies belong to Pat Jennings and Steve Heighway in a Liverpool v. Spurs match in 1973. Keeper Jennings came off worst. He damaged his ribs

of football is low, and the best teams don't always win. Nor do the best footballers stand out.

Often very ordinary club players may star. Trevor Hockey, who won nine caps for Wales, is one instance. Derek Spence of Northern Ireland is another. What trouble Spence gave our defence one sunny afternoon in Belfast in May 1975! No one at the back, which included such sound performers as Dave Watson, Colin Todd and Emlyn Hughes, dared relax for an instant against this blond centre forward. We were mightily relieved to finish with a goalless draw after a display by Spence that was typical of the club footballer being inspired by a whiff of the big-time and playing above himself. He must have felt, 'Here I am, a Third Division player with Bury, presented with a great opportunity. If I do well against England, someone must come for me.'

Certainly Spence did not look out of place in First Division company that day, but the big clubs kept out of the bidding. Only Blackpool came for him, and they sold him later to a Greek club for a year before buying him back for £50,000. The top scouts, who had refused to be over-impressed by a one-off show, probably nodded knowingly.

Another drawback to the home international series is what I call the 'treason factor'. In all the camps players' tiniest weaknesses are being revealed by club-mates to men who will be opposing them in League matches a few months later. I was asked in Dublin, 'What does Steve Heighway do?' and started saying, 'Well, he has a funny way of beating you by dragging the ball on his left foot . . .' Even as I was talking, and no longer connected with Liverpool, it was hard not to feel that I was letting Steve down.

Trevor Francis raised the same point after an England penalty contest. We were trying to elect a new penalty-king by organizing a shoot-out between five players who took penalties for their clubs. Francis complained to me afterwards, 'It's all wrong, I can't agree with this. I have just taken six penalties against Joe Corrigan who now knows everything I do from the spot; that knowledge could cost my club a goal if I have to take one against him in the League.'

The build-up for the home series is wrong, too. It is nothing but leg-pulling at the clubs for weeks beforehand. The back-chat at Liverpool between myself and John Toshack of Wales must have been echoed in dressing rooms throughout the League. I never missed any opportunity before an England-Wales game to remind him of my part in his club goals.

'Won't have K.K. laying 'em on like that for you next week,' I would say. 'Going to be too busy down the other end.'

Tosh would pretend not to hear but, when a ball went in, might turn and inquire, 'Wouldn't that look handsome in the Wembley nets, Kevin?'

The Welsh are very nationalistic, and very proud of their country. I know from two years of living among them how they stoke themselves up for matches against England. They have a word for it, 'hwyl', which I think means fervour.

The first million-pound Briton Trevor Francis playing one of his last games for Birmingham City before being sold to Nottingham Forest in 1979

The English attitude – or arrogance, if you like – is: 'We're being set up here, with everything to lose and nothing to gain.' Our team tends to feel rather like a champion compelled to meet a club player for a worthless prize; the champ would rather not be in that position, yet has to play.

England's outlook is different against the Scots, for then the Scots are the ones who feel superior. They see themselves as the master-race of football; all their players are blessed with genius and their teams never have bad spells. No chance is wasted, either, to remind us that Scotland qualified for the last two World Cups, while we didn't. Useless trying to point out that they were first-round failures in West Germany and in Argentina. The Scottish mentality has already transformed those disasters into triumphs. 'Only unbeaten side in the 1974 World Cup,' they boast, adding, 'Only lost once in Argentina and we beat the finalists, Holland. Not a bad record!'

The Scots are marvellous to play with, but hell to play against. They treat the game as war. They are also cruel mickey-takers, always stirring it up – yet the first time I was in a squad against Scotland, on 14 February 1973, the ridiculing was done by us. The match, in which Bobby Moore won his hundredth cap, was staged to mark the Scottish F.A.'s centenary but turned into an anniversary party they now prefer to forget. England caught them on a slippery pitch at Hampden Park and scored three goals in the opening quarter of an hour; the final score was 5-0.

Some of our lads, reminded in the programme that the series began on a cricket pitch at Partick in 1872, greeted the Scottish substitute in John Arlott tones: 'Here comes Stein from the pavilion

My favourite footballer – Mick Channon of England beating a slide-tackle by Malcolm Page of Wales. Wembley, 1975. The score was 2-2

end.' Willie Morgan had gone off injured, accompanied by a stinging lack of sympathy from a team-mate who was heard to say, 'Ye're a fly wee fellow, ye must know we're in for a drubbing.'

That night the English players vied for who could mimic the daftest Scottish accent as they quoted and re-quoted a vainglorious preview from the *Glasgow Herald*: 'We must continually remind the English that they can manage only a rustic and inadequate imitation of football's glories.'

The Scots got their own back four years later, on 4 June 1977, in what, although we didn't know it then, was Don Revie's last match at Wembley as England manager. I had a dead leg and could not play, so I sat and watched us lose 2–1. The result made a bit of miserable history as the first time that England had lost two successive matches at Wembley, Wales having won 1–0 there earlier in the week.

Scotland were better balanced that day. We looked a team of strangers, and I remember some slack marking at a dead-ball kick on the left when Gordon McQueen scored their first goal. My most vivid memory, though, is of the blue and tartan bonnets swarming out of the stands and terraces to invade the pitch at the final whistle and start dismantling Wembley bit by bit. They looted the goal posts and the crossbars, the nets and the corner flags. They whipped out dirks from their kilts and cut out the penalty spots for souvenirs, then they began carving up keepsake patches of turf. Almost the only things left were the twin towers. After years of believing 'It can't happen here', the Football Association ordered fences for all future Wembley matches.

The Scots in that 1977 invasion were good-humoured rather than malicious, celebrating rather than wreaking revenge. Yet the sheer numbers, maybe 60,000 tumbling and dancing on the pitch, were a terrifying sight. I was on foot in the tunnel, anxious to join our lads but unable to see anything. I waited ages for the police, marching line abreast, to clear the ground because I didn't dare to walk through the mob.

The invasion demonstrated yet again that no one has any precise idea how many Scots turn up in London every two years for the big game. They are allocated 30,000 tickets and somehow lay their hands on about 70,000; it would not surprise me to learn that a further 70,000 come along for the ride. In the days when Covent Garden pubs opened at five in the morning it was a commonplace at breakfast time to find legless Scots clutching the lamp-posts in Long Acre and Bow Street while the unconscious fans slumped in shop doorways. We used to go to the cinema on the Friday night, and there was always a Jock-spotting competition on the England bus. Points were awarded for varying degrees of helplessness; some we saw not only could never have recovered in time to reach Wembley but probably stayed unaware of the score until Sunday.

I am not a Jock-hater and my best mate at Liverpool, until his transfer to Bristol City, was Peter Cormack from Edinburgh. What's more, I admire the Scots as wonderful supporters of their own players. For the rest of us, they are a security risk.

Welsh crowds are not normally troublesome but I was kicked at Cardiff in a pitch invasion, whacked on the leg with enough force to stagger me over the line. The assailant was a kid who had run on with a gang of ordinary cheerful youngsters only wanting to pat players on the back. Would the Scots have stopped at a kick? There is no denying that some of them turn foul-tempered in drink. All it needed — so ran my thoughts in the tunnel — was one lunatic to hit me over the head with a bottle, or to stick a knife in.

Scottish fans on the rampage at Wembley after winning 2–1 in 1977. They took both goals, the nets, and dug out patches of turf for souvenirs

It was in May 1975, before a game against Northern Ireland, that I actually received a death threat – supposedly from the I.R.A., in fact it was before that game I always think of as 'Spence's match'. England had not played in Belfast for a few years because of the troubles, but eventually we agreed to go. And that is when two letters were received, one at the Football Association offices in Lancaster Gate, London, and the other by a member of the F.A. Council. I knew nothing about them until Don Revie drew me aside two days before we were due to fly and said, 'Would you fancy a weekend at home with your wife?'

I asked what he meant, and he said, 'You're in the team, don't worry about that, but we've had a death threat against you if you set foot in Ireland.'

I went up to my room and phoned Jean, my wife, who said she would prefer me not to go.

'There's no way I'm pulling out,' I told her. 'Some silly bugger in Ireland is trying to pick an England team.'

So she just said, 'I won't rest until you're back', knowing argument was useless because I'm the sort of person who never goes back on a decision. Once my mind is made up, I do it. Right or wrong, I do it.

Death threats and ill-wishes are not what I expect from Ireland. I am shocked by it because there is Irish in me, and I like the Irish as a nation of talkers and charmers and individualists. You probably know the saying 'Liverpool is the capital of Ireland'; certainly, every weekend they come over by the boatload to watch the lads at Anfield. Funnily, though, the club never seemed to sign players from Northern Ireland in my time.

The first time I played international football in Ireland was under that death threat in Belfast. I already had eleven caps and was starting to believe that I had almost made it as an England player, and the team was building a run of six consecutive clean-sheets – struggling clean-sheets, some of them, but that is often how long runs start. With workmanlike, not brilliant, performances.

I was believing in myself because Don Revie believed in me. A week earlier, on the bus back from a European championship victory in Cyprus, he sidled up to say, 'Thanks, wee man. You gave me everything today.' I glowed, thinking, 'At last, here is a manager who appreciates work-rate.' For the basis of my game is work-rate, although international purists tend to pooh-pooh it while lavishing praise on the stylists, those elegant ones who pull balls down in the classical manner and then knock the pass through with a text-book left foot.

Yet what happened to me after being commended in Cyprus and going to Belfast despite that death threat? I was left out without a word from Revie. The match was against Wales, on 21 May 1975; I expected to play and I was not picked. So I went home. I walked out.

The public were not on my side this time; 'Little baby has gone home to his mum' summed up their attitude. In fact, my mother was in Doncaster, my wife was in Cornwall and I had gone home alone to an empty house in Wales. The press were outside and I was like a prisoner. It was a horrible experience and yet I still maintain that, in a way, I was right. A player being left out is owed an explanation by the manager because being dropped is such a blow. No club manager would dream of leaving anyone out of a League side without first saying, 'Look, son, don't worry but . . .', and that type of soothing reassurance is even more important in international squads.

Revie explained when I returned that he was only resting me against Wales because he wanted me fresh, eager and going for the win against Scotland on the Saturday. I said, 'If you had only said so earlier I wouldn't have caused you such a problem.' Thank God Revie did bring me back immediately (and it took guts to do so) or I probably wouldn't be where I am today. A side-effect of all this was an increased determination on my part to play my best for England because, sensing that I had lost the fans' esteem, I felt that a couple of bad games might shove me into obscurity.

Happily, my return coincided with the kind of scoreline that gives all Englishmen a rosy glow: England 5, Scotland 1. Their goalkeeper had a nightmare time; he was too late for everything. Even I could have stopped one of the two goals by Gerry Francis. I scored one myself, and I made one, heading Alan Ball's free kick against the bar for someone, either Kevin Beattie or Colin Bell, to stab in from two yards. We played super football, Gerry Francis had his best game for England, and we all thought, 'This side can't be changed.'

But because it was the end of the season and there

David Johnson, my old Liverpool clubmate, playing for England in 1975 and starting to twist through the double Scottish challenge of Frank Munro (No. 4) and Danny McGrain

was no summer tour, Revie did change it in the four months before the next match. Ball was dropped, never to play with England again. It hurt him deeply.

At the centenary match against Wales on 24 March 1976 I captained England, and this was followed by a victory at Cardiff where Peter Taylor scored a great twenty-yarder; then, on 11 May, we beat Northern Ireland 4-0, with me in midfield for the first time.

Players cannot pick their own positions in a team; besides, I am happy to play anywhere, any time, for England – but given a choice I would plump for midfield. There I can be useful as the linkman who influences what comes through from midfield, instead of being only someone on the end of attacks and reliant on others. Liverpool and Hamburg always arranged that I drop back a little in away matches; at home, I pushed right up. That is the ideal balance for me.

I stayed in midfield for England's next game, four days later, the result of which knocked me flat. We lost at Hampden Park after being a goal ahead. I hate losing to Scotland, but that was not all: Ray Clemence, who I had seen make only one previous mistake in six years, let Kenny Dalglish stick the winning shot through his legs. No chance of Scottish fans allowing Ray to forget that one! A year later I saw a banner hoisted on the Wembley terraces showing a goalkeeper doing ungainly splits under the slogan 'Spread 'em, Ray'. Anyway, at Hampden there was a general apology in the dressing room from Ray. Even as he spoke, I knew we wouldn't see him again for a few days.

After the defeat in Scotland I played only two internationals against opposition from the British Isles over the next two years. This was partly because of injury, but mostly because Hamburg needed me for a summer tour.

The two games were at Wembley, and I prefer to draw a veil over our showing against the Irish Republic. They gave us an exhibition, while we were terrible. The other was against Wales yet again, on 31 May 1977, when a penalty by Leighton James gave them their first postwar victory in England. Great for Welsh fans, who can warm themselves for years on that result.

English fans, less obsessed with the home series, fix their eyes on the bigger game overseas. That's why no England appearance excited me until I faced a team from outside the British Isles, a team with a striker who is now world-famous.

4 Against the World

Mario Kempes played in my first match against a foreign country, yet I barely remember him. He didn't stand out, and I say that even though the scoreline – England 2, Argentina 2 – apparently contradicts me. For Kempes scored their goals, the second being a last-minute penalty awarded by the Argentinian referee who was travelling with them to the World Cup in West Germany.

That alone tells you a lot about Kempes and the Argentinian view of him. He was only nineteen, only in his third international match and having his first sight of Wembley, a stadium whose renown has buckled the knees of many older and more experienced footballers. Yet the team turned to him for a spot-kick that meant the difference between saving face and an unwelcome defeat.

Hugo Ayala, a long-haired streak of greased lightning, is the Argentinian I remember most vividly from that match. 'Good God,' I thought, 'there can't be anybody quicker on a football field than this fellow.' Ayala, although only twenty-eight, seemed to have dropped out of the squad by the last World Cup. Kempes, still only twenty-three when collecting his winner's medal at River Plate stadium, had taken over as The Man. Jackie Charlton and Ian St John, who had been in Buenos Aires working for T.V., returned with a snatch of

song that had caught on with customers in the city's British pub. To the tune of Camptown Races, it ran: 'Who put the ball in the Dutchmen's net? Kempes, Kempes!'

Johan Cruyff, the greatest Dutch footballer of all time, wouldn't think that ditty funny, any more than he would vote for Kempes as the new number one player of the world. 'He's not as good as he looks,' Cruyff said to me when we discussed Kempes that summer, adding, 'Although there's no denying that he's had a great World Cup.' Cruyff's judgment was obviously drawn from his experiences with Barcelona in the Spanish League, where Kempes plays for Valencia.

Left : 'Never mind the ball, play the man' – or how Cerezo of Brazil stopped me with a foul during the 1–1 draw at Wembley in 1978

Right : The 1978 World Cup final, with Mario Kempes of Argentina losing the ball to one of Holland's van der Kerkhof twins. It's Willy

But I wasn't assessing Kempes as a club footballer, only as a World Cup player, and there, I thought, he was the master card, the difference between Argentina and the rest. He is fast, skilful, brave and very deceptive for defenders in the way he drags the ball under his left foot. Kempes does the business where it counts – in the box. He stuck away some fabulous goals. Fortunately for me, his nationality makes him ineligible for nomination as European Footballer of the Year. Had he been in the running, I could not have won the title – at least, not for 1978.

Experience is gained so young and so fast in football that my first match against foreigners seems a lifetime ago. After less than six years of playing against the world I feel confident about issuing this challenge: 'Put any international team in the world on a pitch and, if you like, disguise their strip. And I will bet that after five minutes of studying their play I will name their nationality – and be right nine times out of ten.'

It seems to me that the character and mentality of a nation is often revealed in its football team. Look at East Germany, one of the most bureaucratic Communist countries. Until FIFA changed the rules to stop them, the East Germans used to send on a whole committee to treat every knock. The moment a player went down, teams of doctors and officials ran across the touchline. Well, they didn't really run. They were too burdened with their equipment for that.

For three or four years I felt the Russians might emerge with a really good team. But they never have, and probably never will, because their players are robots. If playing styles reflect a nation's life, then theirs is regimented.

Mario Kempes in the 1978 World Cup final infiltrating between Willy van der Kerkhof and young Erny Brandts (No. 22)

Behind the Iron Curtain is the place to test an England player's mettle. There's not one Communist country where I have ever wanted to spend an hour longer than necessary. It's a different world, with its depressing cities. And in the Slav lands they have a different alphabet, which means you can't even start to guess the meanings of signs, let alone the headlines on the sports pages. I don't want to mention names but I've seen England players not compete in places like Russia, Poland and Czechoslovakia. I've seen the faces of players known as stars at Wembley but the legs and the heart belonged to someone else, a very ordinary someone else.

If I ever had to pick an England team to come back with both points from Leningrad, it would not include any of our homers. These are the lads whose talent – which can be enormous – wilts in any hostile atmosphere. It's a little flaw in their character and, as you climb the ladder of international football, every little flaw is magnified. That's the reason why some very gifted footballers win so few caps.

At Wembley, you know that if the opposition chop you down you'll get a free kick. If they chop you a couple of times, they'll be booked. But away from home you never know how many kicks you may have to endure before the assailant is warned – never mind booked. That's why managers – and rightly, too – stick by players of battle-tested bravery, experienced men. Experience is the commodity that money can't buy – although it can buy almost everything else, even behind the Iron Curtain.

The poor old pound sterling may be struggling to stay out of the Western relegation zone, but it's still

In training for the 1978 friendly against Hungary

highly prized in Communist countries. In one of the government shops in Poland, I bought what seemed like a hundred pounds worth of presents for just a couple of fivers. And the experience of a pressman in Prague has become an England legend. Currency spivs, who lurk round hotels reserved for foreigners, offered him their usual terms for a pound, five times the official Czech rate. He said, 'No, eight times.'

'Never,' said the spivs. 'You steal the bread from our children's mouths.'

'Eight times,' insisted our man. 'Or no business.'

Eventually the spivs caved in. Or so they said at a secret meeting in the Englishman's room. He handed over £20, and they tipped a mountain of koruns on to his bed. The reporter, a generous soul, was not seeking profit for himself; he intended to treat everyone in the party. Soon he came down with armfuls of koruns, plonking them on the bar and ordering champagne all round. The bar-man sprang into action, then something made him pause. He walked back to inspect the notes, then burst out laughing at the swastikas and engravings of Hitler. The spivs had paid in worthless Nazi occupation money.

The Dutch are one of my favourite football nations but so cash-conscious. Always before World Cups, Holland's major problems are not over selection, individual form or tactics but over how much money they are going to make. Their footballers are clever, several of them speak half a dozen languages, and they are honest to the point of bluntness – as on that night in February 1977 when they gave us such a going-over at Wembley.

I know Johan Cruyff pretty well, I've played against Johan Neeskens, and I have played with Wim Suurbier and Johnny Rep in a European showpiece match. Rep was always matey and, after only ten minutes at Wembley, he said as we walked past each other in midfield, 'Kevvy [he could never

I've called the Russians a set of robots. Look at this picture of their team and see if you agree

Three stars from one of the most fluid and attractive sides of my time – the Dutch 1974 World Cup team. On the left, Johnny Rep. On the right, Johan Neeskens. And foreground (where else?) the marvellous Johan Cruyff

manage the "n"] this is the worst England side I have seen. You have problems here.'

That was with the score 0–0 and the game barely started. As he walked away, I thought, 'How can he see that already?' Holland took us to pieces. They beat us 2–0 and we couldn't have complained if it had been 10–0. They were a class ahead of us. Rep had sized us up immediately, which is typical of Dutch intelligence. They are bright, all their players. There is an air about them, an arrogance that is not offensive.

Isn't it staggering that a little country of 10 million people fields the best tactical side in the world? They have incredible skill in tutoring players and then blending them into teams. Back at the hotel, it can be all uproars and splits and arguments about bonuses. But when the Dutch walk into the tunnel they turn into a team. I thought that was a marvellous achievement by Holland in Argentina to reach the World Cup final again. They were without Cruyff and had some moderate players, but they are fighters; they kept together and worked. I suspect the Dutch enjoy critics saying, 'You can't play, you haven't quite got it', because then they decide, 'We'll show 'em.' That's their character, and I like it.

The Yugoslavs are another fascinating race. It's frightening just to see them warm up. They have exceptional ability and technique, they are flashy and love to show off. I train under a Yugoslav, Branko Zebec, at Hamburg and play with another, Ivan Buljan. Their outlook is identical: they hate anything easy. In a simple situation requiring only a straightforward pass, our Yugoslav player will always try something fantastic. The easy way does not interest Ivan; what he loves is being plunged into an apparently impossible plight. That gives him a chance to perform.

That national mentality probably explains how Yugoslavia, when only ninety minutes from qualifying for Argentina, threw away their World Cup place to Spain. It didn't surprise me that Yugoslavia won the important Monaco youth tournament last year. I would back them to beat any kids in the world, but there's a barrier that stops them developing further, and that's their own nature. They remind me of the Scots in that they are their own worst enemies, hooked on self-destruction.

The German outlook is serious and earnest: 'Run hard, work hard, fight hard and you'll reap the rewards.' The Slav attitude baffles them, as it does me.

Johan Neeskens scores a penalty against Bulgaria in the 1974 World Cup. The ground: Dortmund. The result: 4–1 for Holland

Above : Tussle at the River Plate – Leo Luque of Argentina (in the stripes) and Arie Haan of Holland during the 1978 World Cup final

Below : Gerd 'Der Bomber' Muller takes off at Munich in the 1974 World Cup final, but Dutch keeper Jan Jongbloed is positioned to save

For the simple goal, there has never been anyone better than Gerd Muller of Bayern Munich and West Germany. 'Der Bomber', they called him, although probably not one of his goals, and there are over 600 of them, has been explosive. He is dumpy, a funny build for a centre forward, and he is always scoring the same goals. Through a defender's legs, or rolled past an unsighted keeper, the sort of simple little goals that you think a kid in the park could score. But Muller does it every week.

I wonder what a foreigner might deduce about life in England from our football. Nothing complimentary, I imagine, because they all think we are too physical. That's why Italians and Brazilians, whose own game is not kick, hustle and buffet, come and chop us. They are scared of not matching us physically and, as a result, overdo it a bit themselves.

We played super stuff against Brazil at Wembley only to get chopped down. My love affair with Brazilian football ended that night – although it must be said that our crowd provoked them by booing their anthem. Touch football is the name of the game for those gold shirts. They are quite genuinely horrified when a big bloke like Dave Watson barges through, going 'Buff!', or when they are brushed aside in challenges. They combat that with some wicked fouls.

Two myths persist over here about Brazilian football: that they can pick an international team from the thousands of beach footballers, and that they never work at any part of the game except ball skills. Even the briefest glance into their headquarters would explode these myths. They fill a wing of a hotel with enough weight-training gear to satisfy Samson, and team manager Claudio Coutinho, perhaps more of a fitness expert than a football man, ensures that everyone uses it. Coutinho, who is fluent in English, raised a quizzical eyebrow when someone mentioned the ball-artists on the beaches. 'Too slow, every one of them,' he said. His English listeners were flattered to hear that he looked to us for inspiration. 'I read *World Soccer*,' he said, 'and the F.A. *Guide to Coaching* is by my bed. I read it regularly, I like the ideas. The English have good ideas and vision, I think your football will be re-born.'

National managers who imagine they are under pressure from the fans ought to try a season in Coutinho's shoes. Our 0-0 draw with Brazil in November 1977 was regarded as a disaster, and during the 1978 World Cup his effigy was burned in the streets, although Coutinho's team were third-place winners.

The Italians react to the English game in the same way as the Brazilians, although, contrary to what some people imagine, they did not put an immense amount of stick about in that World Cup qualifier at Wembley in November 1977. Even so I had a couple of clashes with Romeo Benetti. He began it by digging his elbow on to the top of my head – which he could do because he is taller than I am, as are most people. I retaliated with my elbow, catching him flush in the mouth. A bullseye because one of his front teeth shot out. He gave me a look that could kill and said in broken English,

Power in the air, as shown by Dave Watson in heading clear against Brazil at Wembley

Claudio Coutinho had his effigy burned in the streets of
Rio, even though his Brazil team were third-place winners
in the 1978 World Cup

Kasiu Deyna, 1974 Polish World Cup captain, who has
struggled to adjust to English pace since joining Manchester
City in 1978

Osvaldo Ardiles of Argentina and Tottenham celebrates his first goal in England. The victim: Derby keeper Dave McKellar

'I get you, Keegan. Before finish.' Then he spat at me, and it took ages to clear my eye. But as the game wore on, with me still running too fast for him, I thought confidently, 'You won't get me, chum.' He did, though.

It was when I laid on the goal for Trevor Brooking. The T.V. replay confirms my impression on the field: Benetti waited, letting me knock the pass through and then coming in high. He whacked me so hard that my knee ballooned, and I had to go off. That was the price of one tooth, and perhaps the price modern England players are paying for the days of Stiles and Storey.

Continentals accuse us of putting too much emphasis on physique and stamina; my time in Germany has brought me round to seeing their point of view. Our football is 'Hurry, scurry, tighten down.' I used to argue with the Germans: 'How can it be too physical? I've played up front all my life and never had a bad injury.' Now I understand their use of the word 'physical'. They don't mean that English football is dirty, but that it's too fast, too competitive, too hard.

That's why a Pole like Kasiu Deyna at Manchester City and a Dutchman like Arnold Muhren at Ipswich found it more difficult to adapt than did a South American at Tottenham. Osvaldo Ardiles was accustomed to pace; it was an important part of Argentina's game in the World Cup. But Deyna, at thirty-one, struggled for the lung-power needed in the English League. And Muhren, though his left foot can make the ball talk, found our speed a problem at first; also the English habit of battling out matches over a twenty-yard patch around the centre circle. In Holland, as in Germany, the midfield is left open.

Every Continental joining an English club is going to miss the warm-up. I didn't want to warm up when I first signed for Hamburg; it seemed stupid, twenty minutes of energy wasted. Now I am programmed to it. The game is alive from the first minute after a warm-up; you are not sighing, 'Oh, if only I'd had that chance after a quarter of an hour, instead of at the start.' A German team warm-up leaves no one with that excuse. You are on the field already sweating and if a chance comes along after two minutes you will stick it in. If you miss, you might have missed it anyway. The sooner Football League clubs warm up, the better for English football. We tend to be complacent, saying 'there's not much wrong with our way' – but our coaches only tinker with warm-ups, they never do it thoroughly like the Continentals. Every week English players do warm-up exercises on slippery floors while wearing studs; it's a miracle there are not more accidents.

We don't seem to understand that foreigners can be ahead of us. We gave football to the world but the Hungarians in 1953, followed by the Brazilians and now the Argentinians, have shown how to develop it.

Joy in 1966. Sir Alf Ramsey, Bobby Moore and Nobby Stiles (still with his teeth out) and the old World Cup

5 Managers

Sir Walter Winterbottom was the first professional to run the England football team, and there have been four other managers since he resigned in 1962: Sir Alf Ramsey, Joe Mercer, Don Revie and Ron Greenwood. I have played for each of those four, a distinction that is shared only by Ray Clemence, Peter Shilton, Emlyn Hughes, Dave Watson, Trevor Brooking and Mick Channon. In full international matches, that is.

I wonder if Brian Clough, the so-called people's choice, will ever manage England. I think he is probably unsuited to the job. Verbally, he is always likely to go over the top. 'I won't speak to any cheating bastards. With cheats and bastards I will not speak,' he shouted through an open dressing room door to Italian sportswriters in Turin after Derby County lost the first leg of a European Cup semi-final. That was some years back, as was his disgraceful speech at a dinner honouring Peter Lorimer of Leeds United. Maybe Clough has changed in the meantime; somehow I don't think so. He can try to hide that uncontrolled side of his character, he can stick it in the cupboard for two years, but it will pop out again. For that's the real Clough.

I heard him at Lorimer's dinner, which was packed with sports people and organized to aid Sunshine Coaches, a children's charity. It was meant to be a nice evening, a time to be particularly pleasant to people because we were enjoying ourselves and doing good at the same time. And then Clough stood up. Instead of proposing the toast, he announced, 'I'm off to the lavatory' –

although he didn't put it that genteelly – and he didn't return for nearly a quarter of an hour. It still amazes me how patiently everyone waited. The toast was 'Peter Lorimer, Yorkshire sports personality of the Year' and, regardless of whether he thought Lorimer deserved the award or not, Clough had agreed to propose it. But his speech criticized Lorimer, the Leeds United club, and the Leeds players.

I was on a big table in a party that included Steve Heighway. We had a bottle of wine – what

Here's a group from the archives – Sir Walter Winterbottom and the England team of 1959. There's Brian Clough (fourth from the left), Don Howe (sixth from left) and, at the far right, Bobby Charlton and Jimmy Greaves. The match was against Sweden at Wembley, and England lost. Centre-forward Clough was never capped again

the hell, it was Sunday night! But Clough picked on us, too: 'If you were my players, those glasses would be swept away,' he said, or words to that effect. Liverpool's next match was a week off, and I don't need Brian Clough to tell me what I can do on a Sunday night when there is no game until next Saturday.

I decided that night, 'I am never going to like this man, I can never forgive him.' Now, through working with Clough on I.T.V.'s World Cup panel of experts last year, I have discovered his likeable side – but only after first running into the abrasive side.

Clough has a knack of rubbing up people the wrong way, as he did me because I had joined Hamburg. 'Well, young man,' he drawled, so patronizingly, 'who have you bet your deutsch-marks on for the World Cup?'

He ribbed me for leaving England; he started ribbing me because my wife was having our baby in Germany. Then I asked him, 'That terrific suntan of yours, you didn't get that by being patriotic. That didn't come from Bournemouth, did it?' As soon as I stuck up for myself he thawed, and even began talking of signing me one day.

Well, one day I would like to play for Brian Clough, though I don't know if I could take him for more than one make-or-break year. I would warn Clough before signing for him, 'I'm the man you can't gag.' Not for me the embarrassment of Trevor Francis, who had to explain to reporters after his million-pound debut for Nottingham Forest, 'Sorry, I'm not allowed to say anything. The boss won't let me.' All Clough's players are restricted in that way; they are forbidden to answer even the most straightforward questions without his prior approval. That's how football clubs are run in East Germany; Clough's attitude seems almost Communist and I don't agree with it. Gags insult the intelligence of footballers and lower their dignity.

I have benefited as much as any player from free-dom of the press; it's a basic democratic right to be able to say what you think; if Brian Clough ever told me I couldn't speak to the press, I would ask him why not. And if he said, 'Because I don't want you to', I would simply tell him that wasn't a good enough reason. A manager can say about me, 'Keegan was bad today' – that's his right. In the

same way it's my right to talk about incidents in the game.

A manager is entitled to warn his players not to say anything stupid that is going to create a bad atmosphere in the team, or upset one of the lads. Players will accept that; beyond this they should be trusted to use their judgment. I cannot see how a manager can treat his team like kids and then expect them to play like grown men. Yet, although there is an element of fear in it, Clough's players have enormous respect for him. That's why he gets so much out of them and, in his heart, I am sure he loves them.

I enjoyed working with him on the World Cup, although it was hair-raising when he once turned his back on the monitor and talked throughout a match to his journalist pal, Vince Wilson. Cloughie was still warbling away when the studio manager warned, 'One minute to on the air.' We fixed on our microphones and Brian Moore turned to him asking, 'General impressions?' The reply went something like: 'A good match, but they could have tried this, and they ought to have tried that. Oh, and wasn't the fellow unlucky with that shot?'

I was astonished, thinking, 'Hell, he hasn't seen it but you can't argue with him. He's dead right.' Vince Wilson explains that Clough, who was chat-ting about his holidays, kept an ear cocked to memorize any excited passages in the commentary and was able to half-glance at the action replays. Well, I was there, and I prefer the theory that Brian Clough has eyes in the back of his head! What a character he is, or perhaps characters.

Norman Wynne, a Manchester sportswriter who was only slightly acquainted with Clough, felt that his recovery from a major heart attack was speeded and brightened by an encouraging personal letter from the Forest manager. A Grenadier, horribly burned by a car bomb in Ulster, had a phone wheeled to his bedside. Clough, though in the middle of that million-pound deal for Trevor Francis, was calling – because the soldier came from Nottingham and was a Forest fan. He might see a small boy outside the ground and call him over: 'Young man, come here. What's your name? Would you like some autographs?' Next morning he is quite capable of telling the same kid to get lost.

That harsh side of his nature is a handicap, be-cause in other ways Brian Clough stands head and

Brian Clough in the Forest dug-out. A picture that sums up the word 'motivation'

It's a winning line – Forest manager Brian Clough (left), partner Peter Taylor (centre) and their £1,000,000 capture Trevor Francis

shoulders above any present club manager in England. His record of taking two run-of-the-mill Second Division clubs, Derby County and Nottingham Forest, into the European Cup is all the reference he needs. He has an air of obvious ability – although he needs a second opinion on assessing players, which is why he has the partnership with Peter Taylor.

I can't take seriously his talk about retirement at fifty; I cannot imagine Brian Clough on the patio doing crosswords. He won't stop until able to declare: 'My teams have won the European Cup, the Super Cup, the Cupwinners' Cup, the U.E.F.A. Cup, the F.A. Cup, the League Cup twice and the League championship twice.' Then, being a perfectionist, he is likely to add, 'Now we'll win them again, and more decisively!'

Sir Alf Ramsey was in utter contrast to Clough and, indeed, to any other manager I have met. His manner was reserved and public school, he sounded upper-crust and my first reaction was, 'How the hell did he come into football?'

In fact, Alf was the living example of that Bill Shankly wisecrack: 'I had no education, I've had to use my brains.' He left school at fourteen and worked for a time as a grocer's boy. Because of war service he was unable to turn professional until in his mid-twenties.

Ted Bates, a Southampton director and formerly their long-serving former manager and player, was a team-mate on Alf's League debut. He once recalled: 'He came out of the Duke of Cornwall Light Infantry determined to have a go as a footballer, and was always a bit apart from the rest of us. He was a very accurate player, very thoughtful, and would never get into a situation that exposed him. I think he was the same as a manager.'

I was still in a pushchair when Alf played his last game as England's right back, but people remember him as a player who used brains to overcome his deficiencies, which were lack of height and pace. I came in at the end of Alf's reign and so cannot talk with deep knowledge, yet my feelings about him seem to coincide with those of men who knew him for years.

He was clearly highly intelligent, as might be expected of a manager who, in the space of only nine years, had won Third, Second and First Division championships for Ipswich Town and the World Cup for England. He was a compulsive handshaker, always most polite, and yet I sensed that he really didn't give a damn about what other people thought. Pushed enough, he might do the opposite, which bears out the story of the night the whole town of Ipswich launched itself on a mass booze-up to celebrate the championship. Anyone expecting Alf to join was soon disappointed. 'I'm for an early night,' he said, and was reported later tucked up in bed at half past ten.

That was typical of his cool; even more so was the story of Geoff Hurst's first extra-time goal in the 1966 World Cup final – and if you look carefully at film of the reaction of the England bench you'll see what I mean. Everyone has sprung joyfully into the air, Harold Shepherdson, Les Cocker, the doctors; everyone, that is, except Alf, who remains seated trying to follow the play unemotionally – with the inevitable consequences. As Alf has since confided, when Hurst's goal – with all the controversy of was it or wasn't it over the line – bounced down from the bar, the bench tipped up and dumped England's manager on his backside.

Alf was a man who put the job first. At Wembley, for instance, where directors and the stadium's higher officials might hover in the hope of a nod

More passion from the Forest partners, Brian Clough and Peter Taylor. The rather calmer figure on the left is their long-serving trainer-coach Jimmy Gordon, who has followed Clough on his travels from Derby County to Leeds United to Nottingham

Old-timers are requested to place a hand over the caption and see if they can supply the names themselves for this 1949 England team. Here is the answer. Back row (left to right): Willie Watson, Neil Franklin, Bert Williams, Bernard Streten, Alf Ramsey, Johnny Aston. Front row (left to right): Tom Finney, Jack Rowley, Billy Wright, Stan Pearson, Jack Froggatt. Two days after this picture was taken they beat Italy 2-0 at Tottenham

Whack! Geoff Hurst completes his hat-trick in the 1966 World Cup final against West Germany at Wembley

from the great man, Alf is remembered for always sweeping past everyone to seek out the only person of interest to him: the groundsman, Percy Young.

I never felt at ease with Ramsey and yet, another of those contrasts in his character, he was relaxing. Before my first game, he said, 'Go on, off into town. Don't do anything stupid, just relax a little. We'll be serious tomorrow.' He relaxed players, he was a players' man, and he had the authority of someone who has achieved it all: the First and Second division championships as a player in Tottenham's push-and-run team, the club successes as a manager, and then the World Cup. When he entered a room, there was a hush, a feeling of respect. When he spoke everyone listened, and what he said was always commonsense.

Probably no football manager in history has never once upset a player, but if such a paragon exists then his name is Sir Alf Ramsey. Has anyone heard a player slag him? I haven't.

Nor have I ever met anyone with a bad word about Joe Mercer. People say he was the best English left half of his generation, winner of a League championship with Everton and of five successive caps in the season immediately before the war. I can imagine Joe Mercer playing; he would be bubbly and infectious with courage and hope. I can understand why Arsenal bought him

Joe Mercer with the F.A. Cup, hoisted aloft by happy Arsenal team-mates at Wembley in 1950. I'm using this picture even though the losing finalists were Liverpool!

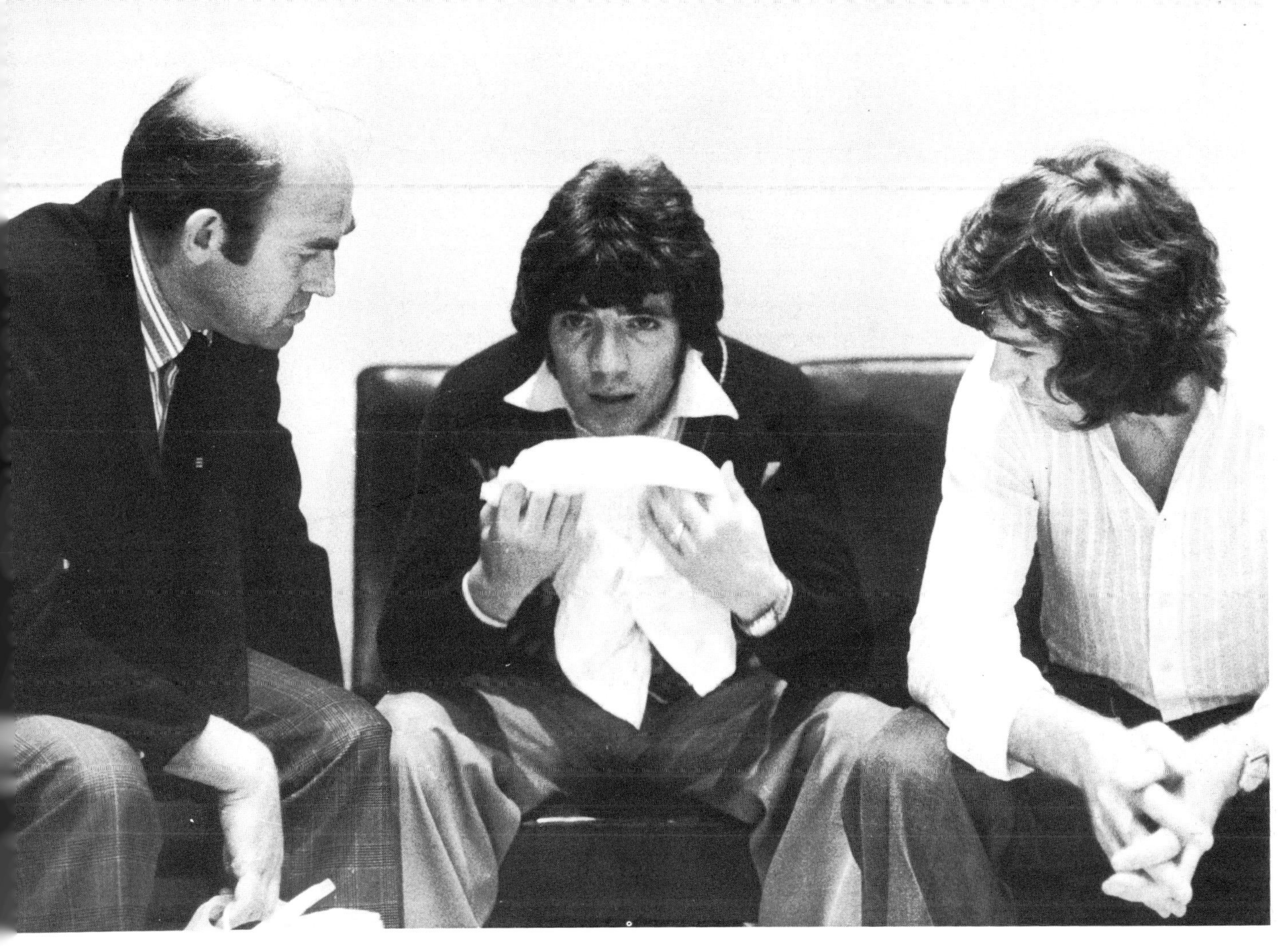

Fed up and far from home – that's me in Belgrade after being beaten up by airport guards in 1974. Dr Neil Phillips (left), then England's medical officer, and Malcom Macdonald offer consolation

after the war, a £7,000 veteran who captained them to two championships. He was still playing in the First Division at thirty-nine; it took a broken leg to stop him. That gameness led him into accepting England's caretaker managership after Alf was sacked in April 1974. The chance had come years too late for Joe, who was entering his sixties.

I remember him ill – with sciatica, I think – in Belgrade after I had been beaten up by the airport guards, and how he calmed an angry meeting of players wanting to fly straight out of Yugoslavia. 'We can all go home, no problem,' said Joe, 'but Kevin won't be able to come with us. He'll have to stay and answer any charges. The only way we'll get him out is by sticking together and answering them back on the field. It's their country off the field, but they can't stop us on it.' Nor did they! That was a smashing speech in the circumstances; indeed, Joe always had a knack for finding the right words. He was able to criticize without condemnation, intent on encouraging, and never snapping, 'That was stupid, what were you thinking of?'

Going on that tour with Joe Mercer was like going on holiday. 'Enjoy it' was his theme. 'You're here because you can play, so go and play. And if you want a beer, then have a beer.' No England team for years had played with such freedom from strain. In his seven games Joe Mercer did our football a lot of good.

6 On Tour with Revie

Don Revie, Joe Mercer's full-time successor, is now portrayed as a national disaster; he has been banned by the Football Association and accused of letting England down and of pulling some strokes when manager of Leeds United. Yet I liked Don Revie. Unpopular and untimely though it may be to say so, I still like him. Too many people talk about his faults while neglecting his strengths. 'Don Readies', a cold man caring only about money, is a crude caricature of the Revie I have seen on the verge of tears in the England dressing room as he exhorted the players.

Revie the player was ending his England career just about the time I was starting at infants' school. He won five of six caps playing inside right to Sir Stanley Matthews. He played with some of the most famous names in England history, not only Matthews, but Tom Finney, Billy Wright of the 105 caps, Duncan Edwards and that other Munich air-crash victim, Tommy Taylor. For a big man, Revie had a subtle touch on the ball and was an outstandingly accurate passer, qualities which fitted him for becoming the first deep centre forward in the League and so giving his name to the 'Revie plan' which took Manchester City to successive F.A. Cup finals in the mid fifties.

I'm just rattling off his record here, never having seen him play, but I can be more first-hand about his career in club management when every domestic honour was won by a club he did not take over

Billy Bremner, ginger dynamo of Leeds United, out training with manager Don Revie

until they were in peril of relegation to the Third Division.

I hated him as Leeds United manager. I played for Liverpool, and I hated everything about our arch-enemies from Leeds. Yet when I met him there was no difficulty about liking him and, as I began to know him, I saw that if I ever became a manager I would be more like Revie than any of the other managers I have known.

He was always glad to help a charity or a good cause, and that's something no one ever tells you about him. When handicapped children or schools came round with a ball for autographing, he would donate three or four more and then go round the lads asking, almost apologetically, 'Would you mind signing?'

People say he wanted the best for himself but I honestly believe his main concern was the best for the players. When he initiated England's contract with the makers of Admiral sportswear, his first comment was, 'Great, now we can pay the players more money.' Because of Revie, we got £300 for a win with England – not a fortune compared with the £1,000 plus paid by West Germany but three times more than we were getting. He said to us, 'Playing for England is an honour, but why the hell should you play for a flat £100 regardless of whether you win, lose or draw.' A £200 win bonus was a little incentive, and in professional sport incentives are important. Players are brought up on them at club level so it's sensible to have them at international level.

His team-talks were sensational. Most people

thought of him as a tactician – perhaps he saw himself that way – but I saw him as a motivator. Sometimes he, and we, would be almost crying. He motivated me. He made me feel I belonged in an England team. He told me to go and help players, to work as hard as I always did while encouraging others to work. He always spoke with deep respect of Liverpool, saying, 'We at Leeds and you at Liverpool', linking the clubs together in a way that suggested that we were the cream. And as he talked the passion would start throbbing through him: 'Come forward, do the things I know you can do. Breathe fire. Pull on that shirt and show the people, put England right up there for them. For God's sake, lads, don't let them down again; make them come and watch us play. Make them proud to sing.'

Some of the lads looked askance when he first produced the England team song, 'It's a grand old team to play for, it's a grand old team to see . . .', but after beating Czechoslovakia 3–0 in his first match we sat in the dressing room singing it over and over again – a full ten minutes after Don had gone out of the room. He wanted the Wembley fans singing 'Land of Hope and Glory' and had the music relayed over the loudspeakers. I think his greatest hope was that one day we would file out of the tunnel and hear the crowd singing it without needing the stereo. This was a side of him that only the players saw.

The bingo and putting sessions were not such a bad idea either; they brought us all into one room on the night before a game, and introduced some competition and incentive. He wanted us together, not disappearing into our rooms. Another likeable thing about Revie was that he was always man enough to admit a mistake, as he did after leaving Emlyn Hughes out for a year and a half. He recalled Emlyn and told him, 'I've been wrong.'

Some gentle training at Wembley in 1975 for (from the left) Alan Ball, Kevin Beattie, Roger Kenyon, physiotherapist Fred Street, and England manager Don Revie

Of course Revie had his faults. I think his greatest mistake was allowing himself to become influenced by the press and, in particular, forging a close alliance with Jeff Powell of the *Daily Mail* and Frank Clough of the *Sun*. It became a team joke: 'We'll read Frank and Jeff in the morning to see if we're in the team.' But it was a bitter joke because their forecasts were so accurate, and resentment grew among the players as we realized that Revie was putting two reporters before the team. The only correct way for an England manager to work is on the basis of sharing information equally around the media while always, absolutely always, informing the players first of impending team changes.

As Revie's captain for a lot of the time, I felt his policy was doomed to disaster. Perhaps I should have gone to him and said so.

But many of Revie's faults, if you think about it, were good qualities carried to extremes. He tried too hard to help everybody, and that caused an argument between us in New York when, quite unasked, he negotiated a television fee for me.

Brian Moore and the Independent T.V. boys asked me whether, as I wasn't playing against Italy, I would mind doing comments for them. I said I would be glad to, if Revie agreed, but when Revie was sounded about it he became very commercial: 'How much are you going to pay him? Will he get the money here?' Eventually, he came to me saying, 'You can do it, and you'll get 500 dollars in cash.' He was genuinely trying to help a player, but I felt he had tarred me and the television people would be thinking, 'Bloody hell, that's a bit steep.' I knew my appearance was not worth £250; I would only be on for about two minutes.

'Thanks, boss,' I said, 'but I don't want you negotiating fees for me. I know you meant well but I have never wanted anybody to do my negotiating, except, maybe, my agent on awkward deals.'

The dossiers provide another example of Revie carrying a good quality to extremes. Before a match he would compile a dossier containing a thorough analysis of opposition tactics, abilities and playing habits. But he would never be content with the broad outline of tactics and style but would want to ferret out every detail on every player. He would watch them, other people would watch them, and the various reports would be amalgamated. You could pick up a dossier and find half a page on a fellow who couldn't play; for good players, there would be three pages.

I never immersed myself in the dossiers, nor did my room-mate Mick Channon. We both felt, without being unprofessional, that our styles could not be altered significantly and so we delved no deeper than the notes on our immediate opponents. The dossiers, which were handed to each player, were useful for that. They were even more useful as scoring pads for cards, which is what Mick and I used them for. It had not occurred to either of us that some of the squad were treating a handy little aid as holy writ – a seriousness never intended by Revie.

We were shocked that the dossiers caused one player to psyche himself out of a match, against Italy on 17 November 1976. Once he walked past in a corridor without recognizing me or responding to a greeting; he kept turning anxiously to the lads, asking, 'Will you come back with me at corners?' I won't reveal his name, it wouldn't be fair because he is still with a big club; besides, as captain for this ill-fated World Cup trip, I felt partly responsible. If only I had been surer of my status as skipper I would have gone to Revie and said, 'That's a result of the dossiers. Burn 'em!'

I can't remember the joke but it was obviously a hit with Mick Channon at the Liverpool and Southampton get-together after the 1976 Charity Shield match

Above : Blocked out in Rome by Cuccureddu of Italy in our 2–0 World Cup defeat in 1976. That's Dino Zoff on the right

Below : Tackling practice for Dave Clement (left) and Trevor Cherry before the Luxembourg game at Wembley in 1977

In fairness, though, he just threw the dossiers into our rooms saying, 'Have a five-minute read on your direct opponent'; he never asked afterwards if we had read it and he never said, 'Memorize it, chew it up, then swallow the bits.'

Not that any single player should be held responsible for our 0–2 defeat by Italy that day, the result that started to block our road to Argentina. The damage was done long before we walked into that unique tunnel at the Olympic Stadium, a telescopic tunnel that extends out towards the centre circle and beyond the range of missile-throwers in the crowd. The damage was done in the selection: England's team that day was the worst technical error of Revie's life.

He picked a back four that had never played together as a block before: Dave Clement, Roy McFarland, Emlyn Hughes and Mick Mills.

His midfield consisted of Trevor Cherry, Brian Greenhoff and Trevor Brooking, which meant two ball-winners who were really back-four men and Brooking as a creator who was still finding his international feet.

Myself, Mick Channon and Stan Bowles were up front, three of us who play exactly the same way. It's no secret that I was always saying to Channon, 'We're too alike as players. We can only play together if I go into midfield.' Stan Bowles was looking for the ball, as I was. The Italians marked man-to-man, they followed us around. We had nobody loose, no wingers, nobody getting away.

The star man was Brian Greenhoff, simply because the Italians let him have the ball. I can almost hear Enzo Bearzot, their manager, giving the instructions: 'Don't let Brooking have the ball, don't let Keegan have it, don't let Bowles have it, don't let Channon have it. But you can let Greenhoff have it, if you've got to.' I think that's why Greenhoff saw so much of the ball. He worked hard for us but the Italians seemed fairly confident that he would not break through and score, although he forced Dino Zoff to save once. The only other England shot to compel a save came from Cherry, who would also have been among the players that the Italians didn't mind seeing with the ball.

I said to Mick Channon before the kick-off, 'I don't think we can win here, the best we can get is a draw. I don't like the shape of our side, the balance is wrong.' It wasn't a real team, it was a defensive line-up but with three front men who could only go forward. Where was the balance? We didn't have midfield men to keep possession because Brian Greenhoff and Trevor Cherry cannot hold the ball. They are defenders.

And Trevor Brooking at that time in his international career – and I don't think he'll mind me saying this – was someone you never saw if we were playing badly. You could always tell how a game was going by looking at Brooking. If we were playing well, he was playing well. That afternoon in Rome he was never in the game; nor was I, nor Stan Bowles, nor Mick Channon. You never saw any of us, we were marked out of it.

Two-nil was a very fair result because that was the worst team ever picked by Don Revie. Yet he had made a balancing error only a month before in the previous international match, on 13 October 1976. We beat Finland 2–1 at Wembley but we were lucky not to lose.

We had won 4–1 in Helsinki during the summer, a great result unappreciated at the time because everyone had deluded themselves that killing off the Finns was bound to be easy. Everyone included Revie, who saw the return match at Wembley as an opportunity to boost our goal difference in the qualifying group to an uncatchable size. He picked

Goran Enckelman, Finland's goalkeeper, beats us all to a high cross at Wembley in 1976

that football monstrosity, 'an attacking team'. Joe Royle was called up as centre forward and Dennis Tueart as the left-winger. We had four men up front, including myself and Mick Channon, and our performance proved once again the foolishness of believing that teams can be designed to score goals by the netful. It's quite possible that the so-called 'attacking team' may not score at all, because the extra strikers get in each other's way. I'm convinced that a normal formation works best against weak opponents because they will present scoring openings anyway.

We were heavy up front that night and too open in midfield, while the players at the back did not push up to fill the gaps. I remember Ray Clemence making a great save when a Finn was clear through and looking certain to put them ahead, and I remember Ray being booked for a professional foul that stopped a certain goal. People were saying afterwards, 'What a bad result, only winning 2–1.'

I told them, 'Just be thankful that we did win, because we didn't deserve to.'

Sometimes it's hard to understand how managers think, how they can complicate a simple game. Teamwork boils down to a couple of sentences: 'When they have the ball, we defend. When we have the ball, we attack.' But it demands a proper balance of skills, with defenders who can play a bit and midfield men who can defend. Unbalanced sides like our team against Italy in Rome, like our team against Finland at Wembley, and like our team against Holland at Wembley on 9 February 1977 cannot produce results.

No one can expect to beat Holland with a formation that includes six back-four men. Over ninety minutes the Dutch will set you too many problems, and you won't set them any. That's what happened when Holland won 2–0 at Wembley. We didn't get into them.

Their Football Association had paid £15,000

Finish for the Finns as I score England's fourth in Helsinki during a World Cup qualifier in 1976

compensation to Barcelona for the release of Cruyff and Neeskens, and they got more than their money's worth from Cruyff. He was brilliant. But Neeskens was wasted in marking me. We were so outclassed, we were never going to score; it was one of those games that you prayed might end twenty minutes early. The only really bad thing about being beaten, however – or, as that night, absolutely annihilated – is not to learn from it. Holland gave us a lesson and it may have been a turning point because, generally speaking, we have improved greatly since.

Yet the way he started off I thought we were going to conquer the world under Revie; perhaps we would have done without the bad luck of losing Colin Bell and Gerry Francis. On 30 October 1974, in our first match after he was appointed, we gave Czechoslovakia an out-and-out hammering at Wembley. Three-nil was the score, and it could have been double figures. They had Masny and Nehoda and Ondrus, big names who might have given us trouble, but they were nothing that night. I would have laughed at anyone forecasting afterwards, 'These Czechs will win the European championship.' Yet they won it! Doesn't that show what success England might have enjoyed if only we had maintained the conviction of our first game?

An unbeaten year went by before we met them again in the qualifying group. It was in Bratislava and we were winning again, in the sense that we had quietened their 58,000 supporters. 'This is going nice, this is,' I thought, but then the fog, which had hung around all afternoon and delayed the kick-off, swirled in thickly off the Danube. Suddenly, both goals were invisible and the match was off, abandoned after seventeen minutes.

We never quite picked up the same rhythm next day, although we took the lead around the first half-hour. Mick Channon scored, a goal I made by cutting between two defenders; I was starting to experiment a little and gaining confidence in myself

Marian Masny, one of the world's most skilful wingers. He wrecked us in Bratislava by making two Czechoslovakian goals in a three-minute spell

A picture to melt a heart of stone, but I don't remember the referee seeing it that way! Bratislava, 1975

as an England player. But we were beaten right at the start of the second half when Masny made two goals in three minutes. The actual lead was lost because of a basic error at corners by Ian Gillard, who was guarding the near post.

Right to the day of his very last game, Don Revie always emphasized to full backs: 'When you take the near post, hold the post and face the corner so that you can attack it. Don't do what Ian Gillard did in Czechoslovakia, don't stand INSIDE the post.' Other markers were also at fault, as Revie conceded, but he insisted: 'Gillard didn't do his job properly. His positioning stopped him getting anywhere near the ball when Nehoda headed in.'

Three weeks later in Lisbon we went out of the European championship through dropping a point to the greatest goal I've seen scored against England. It was an incredibly swerving free kick by Rui Rodrigues of Portugal. Until then I hadn't believed a ball could bend so much. 'A whole four yards,' said Ray Clemence, and none of us challenged his estimate.

So we were down, only to rise again in next to no time. Footballers are such born optimists that we returned singing from our next foreign assignment with our spirits higher than at any time in Don Revie's managership. This was a tournament staged in the United States to celebrate 1976, the bicentennial of American independence.

We could have been excused had we felt tired and irritable, instead. Twelve thousand miles of flying and three extra matches had been tacked on

Allan Clarke trying to escape from a Czech marker at Bratislava in 1975, even though held by a leg and an arm

to the usual long, hard season, and then our plane
home was grounded in Boston by a cracked wind-
screen. That sort of aggravation can cause riots at
Heathrow. The scramble for luggage, the un-
scheduled stop, no definite take-off time, the hustle
for phones to tell welcoming wives 'Sorry, darling.'
Yet our lads laughed and joked with the airport
staff, picked up their bags and walked nearly a mile
in the dark to a half-finished hotel that was shelter-
ing us for the night. On the way we treated America
to a full version of Revie's England song, 'It's a
grand old team to play for' – which, although we
neither knew nor cared, is a straight pinch from the
club anthem of Glasgow Celtic.

The other three teams in the bicentennial tournament were Brazil, Italy and a multi-national collec-
tion of veterans like Pele and Bobby Moore under
the label of 'Team America'. Our first match was
against Brazil at the Los Angeles Coliseum, an
athletics and gridiron football stadium that is ear-
marked for the 1984 Olympic Games.

I was satisfied with the facilities, although the
grass was rather too long. What I didn't like was the
pre-match ceremonial with a massed choir singing
the Brazilian anthem, then a full-length 'God Save
the Queen', followed by the 'Star Spangled Banner'.
It was a wonder, as the crowd was largely Mexican,
that they didn't throw in the Mexican anthem as
well. After the singing, someone presented someone else with something and then we had to listen
to a speech. The least important item seemed to be
the game, yet that was what we wanted to get on
with.

We lost, beaten 0–1 by a shot at the death, and
afterwards everyone said, 'Weren't we super,
didn't we play well?' I could not understand what
they were raving about; I thought we were good
only up to a point. The T.V. highlights later further
convinced me that I had seen England play better
and that too many judgments were being swayed
because the opposition was Brazil on foreign soil,
overlooking the fact that they were a long way from
home, too. Brazil sent on a blond full-back as a
substitute for the second half. Marinho was his
name and he was the trump card. He raised the
game for them.

We missed some chances that day, and I missed
the best one by hitting the goalkeeper from about
four yards. Some people imagined I had frozen,

The day Bobby Moore played against England with Team
America at Philadelphia in the 1976 U.S. bicentennial match

but they were wrong. I had run at Leao, who is
Brazil's World Cup keeper, thinking on these lines:
'Be positive, get through and whack it! Don't be
the clever guy who goes up to goalies saying,
dummy, dummy.' I have played against all the great
goalkeepers in the world, and nine out of ten of
them would have moved as I prepared to shoot.
Leao didn't, and that's why the ball hit him.

They knew of me in Brazil, as they know of everyone who makes a name in Europe, so perhaps Leao
thought, 'This Keegan, he's bound to do something different. I'll wait.' That is probably how it
happened; to me, it was just another lost round in
the unending battle of wits between scorers and
goalkeepers.

If the keeper had been Sepp Maier of West
Germany, then I would have tried something different because Maier would have had a surprise
for me if I had dared do anything normal. Psycho-
logy is vital at this level. The forward thinks,
'Something unusual is needed to beat this fellow',
which is exactly what the keeper wants him to
think. He wants you to try the hard thing, he is
prepared for that, so if you do the simple opposite
then you might score.

After my miss, but not as a result of it, I was left
out for the next match in the tournament – against

The Maracana in Rio de Janeiro. Capacity around 200,000, the world's biggest football ground

Italy at Yankee Stadium, New York City. 'They are in our qualifying group for the World Cup,' said Don Revie, 'so I'm not going to show them my hand.' Mick Channon was appointed captain for the day; he, Dave Clement and Trevor Brooking were the only three of the team to re-appear later for the serious stuff in Rome.

No one is ever happy to give up an England cap, but I realized that it was sound thinking by Revie, and the amazing thing was that our team with six changes and three new caps stuffed the Italians. Yet they cut us to bits in the first half, knocking the ball about, getting people in behind us. They played smashing football on a pitch that did not suit their skills, a baseball ground with the diamond's tracks cutting into some parts of the field and the pitcher's mound in one goal-mouth. I was commenting for T.V. and thinking, 'God, it's going to be six', as we came out two down for the second half. But seven minutes later we had won it: Mick had scored twice and Phil Thompson had got one when coming up for a corner.

A weird result, and one that must have greatly relieved Don Revie, whose normal load of superstitious fears had been worsened by learning that some of the pressmen thought our hotel was haunted. It was out along the Hudson River in Rip van Winkle land, with Sleepy Hollow just down the road and a local team calling themselves the Headless Horsemen. Two reporters experienced poltergeist activity, the most sustained visitation happening to Norman Fox of *The Times* – and you can't disbelieve *The Times*.

He was in the bath when it began. First, the vigorous rustling of a pile of newspapers on his bed. 'Ah, the chambermaid has let herself in,' he thought. But that hardly explained the prolonged rattling that followed, from a source he recognized as an airline bag containing flash-cubes. Nor did it explain the next sound, of steady dragging. He left the bath. No chambermaid; anyway, the door was chained. The papers and airline bag were where he had left them, but his heavy suitcase had been moved to the far end of the room.

Revie, who liked to know everything that happened on an England tour, heard of this incident and asked Norman Fox about it. 'So I told him, and he didn't utter a word,' Norman recalls. 'Nor, although it may have been a coincidence, did he speak to me for the next two days.'

From New York we went by coach along the turnpike to Philadelphia for a match in which my two goals can never be included in the records. For the Football Association ruled that Team America were not international opposition; in other words, it was a nothing game. They had Mike England with his dicky knee – you could take a few liberties against him – and Tommy Smith, who had just flown in from Liverpool and was suffering from jet-lag. And if a sports quiz ever asks, 'Where did Bobby Moore play against England?', then the answer is 'Philadelphia, 1976.' Yet the match was a thrill because I played against Pele, still tremendously fit at nearly thirty-six and demonstrating skills that I would love to copy. I remember his double passes and the elegance as he turned and clipped balls. His legs were like iron; other forwards stick their legs out and you can brush through. When Pele tackles you, it's like running into a wall.

A year later, in June 1977, I played with England in Pele's homeland on the world's largest ground, the Maracana in Rio de Janeiro. It has held 205,000 spectators and I suppose, by that standard, the 77,000 watching us against Brazil almost constituted a boycott. There is no grass on the pitch, or not what I call grass. It is more of a green weed that is allowed to grow so long that our lads were joking, 'No boot money in Rio.' England money – £100 an appearance and £200 a win then – is not high compared with what clubs pay, but there is a perk from the boot manufacturers for having their markings displayed in international games. On the Maracana, though, you sink in so deep that only X-ray cameras could have snapped the stripes.

Les Cocker, the assistant manager, was in charge because Don Revie had stayed behind to spy on Italy again. I thought Les did well, not droning on with a lot of detail, but just saying, 'Go out and enjoy it.' We did enjoy it, and we were really good for the first twenty minutes, when we might have scored four. Then the tiredness started getting into us; the long, tedious flight and the heat and humidity of the tropics took their toll. Brazil were shooting in for the final half-hour, but Ray Clemence was brilliant, and Trevor Cherry made a couple of great stops on the line. The result was a goalless draw.

Players don't always realize how tired they are, they are not always careful about how much they take out of themselves. Your energy is not a bottomless pit. Rio made an offender of me, too, in that respect. I rushed around, eager to see the Sugar Loaf mountain, the beaches of Copacabana and Ipanema, the hill of Corcovado with the famous statue. Christ the Redeemer, they call it. At night, when floodlit, it seems to float on clouds while the outstretched arms bless the city – but some irreverent characters travel with England, and one of them said, 'He's signalled a wide!' The Brazilian players were in a hotel halfway up to the statue, in a place where avocados grew wild outside their windows.

Players who talk freely about pressure games don't know the meaning of the term until they have braved a screeching crowd where we played next, the Boca Juniors stadium in Buenos Aires. They call it 'La Bombonera', the Chocolate Box – but it's not for soft-centres! I have played around the world; I have been in European finals, in F.A. Cup finals and in big games for England, but nowhere have I experienced a passion and hostility comparable with the Boca.

It's virtually a three-sided ground with double-tier stands towering straight up from the touchlines so that the crowd seems to be sitting on top of you – an old-fashioned arrangement which is maybe why it was passed over for the World Cup in Argentina. For a confused moment, because we had never before seen a Buenos Aires ticker-tape welcome, we thought, 'The sun's shining but it's snowing.'

Clouds of torn paper floated down, covering the grass and obscuring all the pitch lines. The crowd hopped up and down, they flung out forty-yard banners, they chanted and shouted at us – and you didn't need any Spanish to understand that the words were unfriendly. How could it be otherwise when Argentinian newspapers were front-paging us as 'The Pirates'? Every grudge was dredged up: the ownership of the Falkland Islands, some dispute over straits near Cape Horn, the sending off at Wembley in 1966 of their captain Antonio Rattin, and Sir Alf Ramsey saying 'Animals'.

Menace was in the air from the moment we landed. This was the time when the new military government were fighting to crush the Montonero guerrillas and dared not permit their opponents such a spectacular success as kidnapping the England football team. They also wanted a security rehearsal for the World Cup. So Ezeiza, the international airport, bristled with guns and our motorcade to the hotel stretched for a quarter of a mile. 'Like Mayday in Moscow,' someone said.

The road had been cleared, all side roads had been blocked, guns pointed from pill-boxes on the verges, and every bridge was guarded by soldiers with handcuffs and rifles. Six police cars with

Never mind that Argentinian tackle, just look at the torn paper on Boca Juniors pitch in 1977!

flashing lights escorted us, and two unmarked cars were full of heavies, men with the kind of eyes that peer down telescopic sights. We had two outriders on big Harley-Davidson bikes, one of them doing rodeo tricks like standing on the saddle or leaning back over the rear-wheel while his feet worked the handle-bars.

For the first time on an England trip, the press bus took precedence over the team. 'We're obviously expendable,' said the reporters – but their position allowed them to see how those jovial outriders operated once the convoy entered the city's busy streets. They turned on the sirens, sped through all the red lights and ordered every im-

peding car to pull aside; anyone slow to obey was likely to receive a lapful of broken glass because the two motor cyclists each wore a metal glove for smashing in drivers' windows. The authorities don't mess around in Argentina, as was further shown when we reached the hotel to find armed detectives at both ends of our bedroom corridor.

The 60,000 screaming spectators at the Boca seemed in keeping with the threatening atmosphere of Buenos Aires, but there are ways of silencing noisy crowds. We found one by scoring in the third minute. It began with a free kick. The ball went to Mick Channon out on the right; he crossed first time for Stuart Pearson to come in fast and score a

Daniel Bertoni of Argentina. He was sent off for punching Trevor Cherry, but the referee sent off Cherry with him

great goal at the post. Argentina equalized with an even smarter free kick, which Bertoni bent in unaided. He made it look so easy.

A picture in a Buenos Aires sports paper next day showed our wall hopelessly out of position, but the camera had been made to lie. The picture had been reversed. Ray Clemence's position was right and our wall was right, even though a lot of midgets, like me, were in it. If our tall players had been in the wall then Bertoni would have chipped the ball into an area where our little men could be beaten in the air.

I was proud of that draw. It was not a supergame but, of course, it was never going to be a showpiece. We had to get in battling, and we did it. One each at the Boca represents a magnificent performance in the circumstances, by which I mean the crowd's gradual overpowering of the Uruguayan referee. When a crisis came, Senor Ramon Barreto flunked it. He was not brave enough to send off Bertoni on his own.

That was the only possible, just decision after a second-half clash between Bertoni and his marker, Trevor Cherry. The Argentinian grew frustrated because he couldn't get past. So, quite unprovoked, he threw a right-hander and knocked out two of Trevor's teeth. Trevor stood there and made no attempt to retaliate, so it was an open-and-shut case for a solo sending off. Bertoni had to go. But a riot might have followed if an Argentinian had gone off alone, and the referee shrank from that. So he sent the innocent Cherry off, too. Don Revie was scathing about the decision but powerless to alter it.

Revie had caught us up in Buenos Aires in time to select and manage the team against Argentina. We had no idea that he had been negotiating secretly with the Arabs, and that our next match would be his last with England. It was across the River Plate at Montevideo – and no, you cannot see a trace of the pocket battleship *Graf Spee*, only the spot where it was scuttled on Hitler's orders. A faceless country, Uruguay. The weather was bitter and the match was a goalless stinker; they were dull, we were weary.

On the flight home, I sensed that something was afoot with Revie. I had felt a closeness to him ever since my walk-out, and I was one of the players in whom he confided. I guessed that he wanted to get out of the job; I didn't realize that, in his own mind, he was out already. He surprised us all by signing for the United Arab Emirates. Looking back on Revie, I think he deserved a more rousing exit than 0-0 in Uruguay. I see him as a man with a great pride in England but so hungry for success that, in a manner of speaking, it killed him.

7 The Team Behind the Team

Above : Ron Greenwood in December 1977 after becoming England manager

Left : The place is Belfast, and the England player is Geoff Hurst. A picture that shows the power of the man

Ron Greenwood was an apprentice signwriter before becoming a professional footballer. He used to paint Wembley, and one of these days I believe he will paint it red. There is bound to be a double-figure victory one day when we all hit form together playing the Greenwood way. His theme is: 'We tried defence for four years, and it didn't work. So let's attack.'

Fans are interested again. They know England will have a go and that goals are almost certain. Two wingers and a positive attitude have restored faith and huge crowds leave their firesides on cold nights to watch us. Just look at the gate figures: 92,000 spectators on a frosty November evening for a friendly against Czechoslovakia; the Northern Ireland fixture last February sold out nearly a month ahead.

The first thing that struck me about Ron Greenwood was that he didn't wear 'British is Best' blinkers. He knows other countries have overtaken us and that we must learn from them; he is the only manager I have heard pointing out that winning the World Cup in 1966 was not an unqualified success. He says:

The Germans set up the Bundesliga on the strength of winning the 1954 World Cup, they progressed. We won, but sat back and did nothing. We were so insular.

I'm talking about the development of young footballers; they are our future, our hope of keeping pace with the rest of the world. But our coaching development was wrong, emphasizing competition and pressure instead of technique. No one can win everything but the attempt may stifle the advancement of young players, and technically good kids were discarded only for not being big and strong enough.

We went through a period where it was regarded as essential to win the ball, to stop people playing, to deny space. We cheated by clattering opponents and this harshness was worn as a feather in our caps – 'Let those buggers come over here and see if they can play.'

As someone who has been rejected for being too small, Greenwood's views struck the right note for me. I also liked the feeling of freedom he generates. We are on trust under him, it's no longer bed at ten as in Don Revie's days. Now you will find the England team in a pub on Sunday nights before a Wednesday match. 'Wander down for a couple of hours; I know you won't make fools of yourselves,' he tells us. It's a privilege, and we discipline ourselves; if a new player did anything stupid all the lads would pounce on him.

I think that Ron Greenwood combines qualities from all his four predecessors. His instructions are crisp and commonsensical like Ramsey's. His approach to football and encouragement of players are reminiscent of Mercer. He tries to be as helpful as Revie and looks for similar skills; and I suppose his Lilleshall background is owed to Sir Walter Winterbottom, founding father of the F.A. coaching scheme.

Greenwood is another England manager whose playing career coincided with my infancy, so I can only say that he is remembered at Chelsea, Bradford, Brentford and Fulham as an unusual centre half for his era, one who sought to use the ball, not just to belt it seventy yards upfield. He also played with Hull City when in the Royal Air Force, but, as with Alf Ramsey and Joe Mercer, the war robbed him of valuable early years.

Every time England step into the tunnel at Wembley he sees two reminders of his early struggles: 'North' and 'South' on the dressing room doors are relics of his signwriting. Also, after retiring with an England 'B' cap in 1952 as his main honour, he nailed up some signs pointing the way that football ought to take.

'The secret of football is space; creating it and using it' – that's the voice of Greenwood. Here are some more of his sayings:

Coaches teach football like advanced mathematics when it should be simple arithmetic.

We are searching for the through-ball, the killer-ball; the one that gets behind the defence.

Spectators have got fed up with seeing a bunch of fit people run about. They want to see skill with it.

His coaching skills landed him the F.A. youth team managership and the Under-23 managership while, as team manager of West Ham, he won the F.A. Cup and the European Cupwinners' Cup. With such a long F.A. connection, including eight years as a member of FIFA's technical committee, the England managership seems a logical progression in his career, though the chance didn't come until he was fifty-six.

There is a lot to be said for maturity in a manager, and certainly the years have given Ron Greenwood time to refine his team announcements into the nicest I have heard. I can do his speech off by heart; it goes:

Well, I've got to say this lads, as I've said before and as I always remind you, I can't pick everybody. I can only pick eleven and I don't want the ones who are left out to think, in any way, that they are being discarded. Remember, we're a family.

Now the team is Peter, Viv, Phil, Dave, Trevor, Ray, Tony Currie, Steve, Kevin, Tony Woodcock and Peter Barnes. Ray Clemence, Emlyn Hughes, Mick Mills, Ray Kennedy and Bob Latchford will sit on the bench, and I would like to thank you all very much for coming.

I'll give the team to the press at twelve to help them with deadlines, and so they can give the game a push tomorrow.

In any team selected from a squad someone is bound to feel disappointed, but Greenwood's reassuring manner convinces the lads that there is another chance, that they will be back again.

Something else that has won over the players is his willingness to hear our ideas; the outstanding instance was on the morning of the World Cup qualifying match against Italy at Wembley in November 1977 where we needed to win by a big score. We were sitting in a circle at the Dame Alice Owen training ground in North London, and the lads not in the team were at the far end warming up the reserve goalkeepers Peter Shilton and Joe Corrigan. 'Let's not be scared, let's play,' the boss began saying, undoubtedly at that stage of the preparations with his tactics laid out in full.

Then it turned into a general discussion, for Greenwood is not the sort of manager who inscribes his plans on tablets of stone. He likes a bit of debate, a consensus in the team, and is willing to weigh up any sensible suggestion. I found myself saying:

Look, boss, we've got to beat them good and not worry overmuch about being beaten ourselves. We can't really be tight defensively, anyway, not with four players up front, so why don't we make Dino Zoff kick out every ball?

Because you know what the Italians love? They like the goalkeeper with time to throw the ball out to the sweeper who gives it him back; then Zoff will roll it out to the left back, who gives it inside, and that way they build up.

Let's push up four. Mark everyone, stick Peter Barnes on the right back and move up Dave Watson in support.

Many managers might have given me the brush-off, offering to talk about the idea but in a tone implying 'Not at any price!' But Ron Greenwood paused and said, 'Mmm, it could work, but it throws a lot of responsibility on Emlyn Hughes.' Every time Watson came up with us, Hughes would be left one against one in any counter-attack. 'How do you feel about that, Emlyn?' asked the boss.

Under the boss's eye – in training watched by Ron Greenwood

Above: A hug from Steve Coppell at Wembley in 1977 after a goal against Italy

Below: I can't remember what I've just done in training, but Ron Greenwood looks delighted

'Not too chuffed, there are a lot of risks attached,' he replied. 'But, as the lads like the idea, I'm prepared to have a go.'

We all realized something different was needed against Italy, and thought ourselves lucky to have a flexible manager who was aware that players, too, have opinions. And I know the boss will listen to us again because the tactic worked like a charm. Zoff, most senior of the world's top goalkeepers, let himself become flustered. So did his defence, probably remembering their unexpected collapse against us in New York. If only Peter Barnes had been able to tuck away one of the little chances that the ploy produced, we might have gone on to score half a dozen and, maybe, to qualify for Argentina against all the odds.

But if our plan had flopped, if the Italians had scored from Zoff's kicks, then we players would have been obliged to own up: 'It was our responsibility, we thought it was right and the manager felt he had to back us.'

The team, off their own bat, changed tactics again in the next Wembley match five months later when Brazil started killing us in midfield because our 4-2-4 system was too rigid. I was in midfield with Tony Currie, recalled by England after three years. Wingers Steve Coppell and Peter Barnes were supposed to come back and help us but, for some reason, didn't do so. On top of that, the Brazilian midfielders Rivelino and Zico cheated by not running back to defend when we moved up for corners. They stayed upfield, waiting for the clearances. For the first twenty-five minutes, I feared we were in for a pasting.

There was no chance to put things right until one of our lads was injured. As the game stopped and we waited for the trainer, I called to Tony Currie and Mick Mills, 'Come here, we've got to sort this out.' Then the others gathered and I said, 'It's crazy what we're doing. We're going to get beat seven or eight unless Stevie and Barnesy work back, and unless someone from the back four moves up to reinforce us. Tony and I aren't getting the ball, and without it we can't play.' Tactical changes are usually made by managers at half-time, but when the players themselves can see what is wrong they are better tackled on the spot. England, though, had not done so for a few years because the team lacked leadership.

There had been so many changes, so many new faces. Some players felt they had no right to tell others what to do, and others weren't playing well enough themselves to have their advice received with any respect. When Bobby Moore was captain, he spoke and you listened. But Bobby's last England match was in 1973, and without him authority had weakened to the point where no one knew whose hand was on the tiller. I could look round the field and think, 'God, he didn't play last time, and that lad there probably won't play next time. And him, he's never played before! The bloke alongside hasn't had a cap for years, that one is just back from injury, and the other fellow shouldn't be in!'

Now that Greenwood has formed a nucleus of regular players, a lot of the lads feel more established and more confident. Stability leads to team-spirit, and that is never easy to create in international sides which are collections of outstanding individuals rather than tight-knit groups. Except on tours, England – or any other national team for that matter – cannot hope to match the closeness of a League team. You can see that after Wembley matches, when everyone wants to get back to their own club. Some of them, like Ray Wilkins during that bad season at Chelsea, probably return regretfully. Time with England is a holiday from club worries.

Greenwood is a great believer in talking privately to players. I've watched him with Wilkins when Chelsea were bottom of the First Division and imagined him saying, 'I know your club is having problems and that you, personally, are not in the best of form, but you have done it for England previously and that's why you are here again. You're not here on sympathy.' It's impossible to overestimate the helpfulness of that kind of approach. England is the greatest thing a player can have going for him during a relegation struggle. Just for a couple of days he is away from long faces and the foot of the table, and he'll go back fresh. All right, he has played in another game but it has been a break. He'll feel invigorated. Managers who complain about losing players to international calls ought to realize that it can be a benefit, too.

Perhaps the shrewdest innovation by Greenwood is the recruitment of notable managers and coaches into an England think-tank. The team was

Les Cocker (left) and Don Revie in Czechoslovakia

Terry Venables signing for Q.P.R. manager Les Allen in 1969; he had been transferred from Tottenham for £70,000. Now Venables is a First Division manager with Crystal Palace

Geoff Hurst, man of many parts, at work in Mayfair as a clothes designer

a one-man band under Sir Alf, and a duet under Don Revie and Les Cocker. Now the full orchestra has assembled with, in no particular order, Ron Greenwood, Bill Taylor, Geoff Hurst, Don Howe, Terry Venables, Bobby Robson and Dave Sexton. And what other cause but England could have got Brian Clough and Peter Taylor involved? It was a pity that the continual clash of youth international fixtures with their Forest commitments made them feel obliged to resign.

England fans possibly don't realize the number of people in the background doing essential jobs for the team. As Greenwood says, 'A club manager does ten jobs for one wage, but with England there is an organization that is a pleasure to work with.' We have not gone to the lengths of the West Germans who travel everywhere with their own chef, but almost every other function is covered.

Every England trip abroad is headed by a delegation of officials like the F.A. chairman, Professor Sir Harold Thompson, and members of the international committee, such as Dick Wragg of Sheffield United, Sir Matt Busby of Manchester United, Peter Swales of Manchester City, Brian Mears of Chelsea, Bert Millichip of West Bromwich Albion and Jack Wiseman of Birmingham City. Then there are the permanent paid officials like Ted Croker, a former Charlton professional who is the secretary of the Football Association, and Alan Odell, the secretary of the F.A.'s international department who has been around the world with England over the last fourteen years.

We were all saddened by the sudden death after a jogging run of our nice medical officer, Peter Burrows. He could beat everyone in the squad at squash and table-tennis, he kept us light-hearted, he could stand endless kidding. Ron Greenwood was always teasing him: 'You do everything else, doc. Why don't you pick the team?' We used to watch him checking through hotel kitchens, being meticulous about the cleanliness and the cooking, and we ribbed him, too. 'This food is hopeless, doc,' we would tell him. 'You'll have to go.' And he would play along, saying, 'Yes, the boss is sure to realize I'm not good enough for the job. I don't know how I got it, anyway.' He is bound to be a

Chelsea chairman Brian Mears, a member of the senior international committee

hard act to follow but successor Vernon Edwards has the right background through long experience with England's youth and Under-21 teams.

Norman Medhurst from Chelsea never gets a headline but does a tremendous job mopping up all the little worries that can distract lads before a game. If you have a problem, see Norman. He always finds time to help.

Fred Street of Arsenal must be the best physiotherapist in the country; I have found him always right in his judgment of injuries. A player with a knock goes to Fred on Monday morning and may hear, 'No way are you doing anything on that until Wednesday morning, then we'll test it. See how it goes.' There is no arguing when he says, 'Forget about playing.' But you know there is a real chance if he says, 'Don't kick a ball until Wednesday night and I think you'll get through.' Sometimes I have reported to England's hotel with injuries so painful that I've wondered, 'Should I go and tell the boss straight away that I'm out?' But, on second thoughts, I ask Fred first in the hope of hearing the verdict: 'You have a good chance of playing if you do as I tell you.' Which I always will, knowing he'll be right.

Then there's 'Brod', the England travel officer, Cyril Broderick, or the human ash-tray as we used to call him until he stopped smoking. We're always winding him up, saying, 'You've got a great life travelling the world, no worries. Anyone wants you, you're never around.' In fact, he's always around and always pleasant in a job that no one in the England party envies. It's not easy organizing a plane-load of people, especially split into four distinct groups: F.A. officials, the team, the journalists and the supporters. So carry on, Brod. When we call the trips 'Cook's cock-ups' it's just a joke.

Administration, travel arrangements, medicine chests, kit rooms and treatment tables are essential back-ups for a football team, but the spectators are paying to see the shop-window. That's where all those coaches come in.

Dave Sexton, although chiefly concerned with the Under-21 side, is one I've talked to a lot. He's a quiet man, with an enormous knowledge of the game. Some people said he wouldn't pull up any trees at Manchester United but he took them to the F.A. Cup Final in May 1979. The knockers also overlooked the fact that Sexton won the F.A. Cup

and European Cupwinners' Cup as manager of Chelsea, and chased Liverpool all the way for the League championship in 1976 when managing Queens Park Rangers. Dave never played international football but he has built up a wide knowledge of international teams. He has attended the German school in Cologne, he followed the World Cups in West Germany and Argentina. He keeps abreast of developments.

Bobby Robson runs our 'B' team and is an obvious contender should the England managership fall vacant again. He has long experience at Ipswich Town and the pedigree of two separate international careers while playing for West Bromwich Albion. First, he was an inside right and then, after a gap of two years, a right half good enough to win a further fifteen caps. He has twenty in all. Once the ice is broken, Bobby Robson is a passionate and fluent speaker about football. He has a dry humour, as in describing his old Fulham teammate George Cohen:

The England team that won the World Cup depended, because it had no wingers, on the running of full backs Ray Wilson and George Cohen.

No right back ever penetrated like George, he would fly past defenders and reach the by-line, where his problems started because his final shot or cross was usually so erratic. I told him one day: 'George, you've hit more photographers than Frank Sinatra.'

Don Howe and Terry Venables are two coaches who interest me a lot. Not from working with them, because I haven't had that privilege, but from conversations about football. They have so much to offer. Howe's right leg is scarred by traces of forty-three stitches and eight silver screws from the playing injury that finished him at only thirty-three. He was a cultured England right back, a ball-user in Ramsey's class, with West Bromwich Albion and with Arsenal. From traction he stepped into a tracksuit, coached Arsenal to the League and F.A. Cup double in 1971, managed West Bromwich for a few seasons and then returned to Highbury as assistant manager – incidentally, one of Greenwood's old posts.

Venables of Crystal Palace is the only manager who mixes fiction with football. He is co-author

Bobby Robson (right), manager of England B and Ipswich Town, at heading practice in his England days. His partner is the legendary Duncan Edwards of Manchester United. Only three months after this picture was taken Edwards died of injuries received in the 1958 Munich air crash

with novelist Gordon Williams of several books, including the private-eye stories that provided the title, characters and plots for the I.T.V. series 'Hazell'. That's a rare distinction, but Terry Venables has one claim to football fame that can never be equalled. He is the only player capped at all five England levels: schoolboy, youth, amateur, under-23 and full international. Unmatchable, of course, because the amateur category is now defunct, never to be revived.

I would like to see Howe and Venables more involved in our preparations, but the problem about single international matches is that there is no opportunity for hard training. We can't come together until Sunday evening and we play on Wednesday; Tuesday is too near the match for heavy work-outs, so Monday has to be the main day. But that only gives time for basic stuff like warm-ups, a fun game and a little work on tactics. Tuesday is more tactics, a bit on finishing and another fun game. Wednesday is for set-pieces, the free kicks and corners.

That's been the routine for all the England managers and, I think, impossible to change. People ask me the difference between English and German coaching and I say, 'They are worlds apart because the Leagues are worlds apart in structure.' In Germany, we play thirty-four League games a season. In England you can play sixty Cup and League matches. The Germans can spend all week in training, improving skills. The English club manager has a game on Wednesday and another on Saturday. What can he do in training? He dare not stage a full practice match in case someone is injured; he dare not order strenuous training in case legs get heavy. There simply isn't time for English clubs or the England team to polish techniques as they would like to do.

Bill Taylor is our trainer. He's good but, as a Scotsman working for England, proficiency cannot save him from terrible ribbing. I played against Bill when he was a full back at Lincoln City and I was a winger at Scunthorpe United. So when Don Revie introduced him to the squad five years ago, I couldn't resist saying, 'I've seen you before but never face-on; only when I've looked back.' For Bill, as I'm sure he'll admit, was no greyhound. He was, though, a backbone-of-the-game honest pro who played in all ten outfield positions with Orient

and Nottingham Forest. That's hard to beat as a way of learning to understand everyone's problems.

His enterprise in going on a study trip to the 1974 World Cup in Germany led to the association with England; he saw a lot of assistant manager Les Cocker in Munich and created such an impression that Don Revie sent for him. 'A victory for Joe Bloggs,' said Bill at the time of his unexpected appointment. 'I've been through the heartbreaks of football.' One such heartbreak happened early this year when he resigned from the number two job at Manchester City, feeling forced out by the arrival of Malcolm Allison. But the heartbreaks Bill meant were in his playing days after coming into the English League from the Edinburgh junior club, Bonnyrigg Rose. Football is a small world, and one of them involved England goalkeeper Peter Shilton. It's a story that Bill Taylor often tells:

I was playing for Forest against Leicester and we were both round the bottom of the League. Matt Gillies, who had been the Leicester manager, was joining Forest, and he was in the stand watching. Late on, still with no score, we got a corner and the ball dropped to me about fifteen yards out with no one to beat but Shilton. I sent him the wrong way and shot, but he stuck out his leg and knocked the ball over the bar off his ankle.

A vital point dropped, and everyone was looking at me and saying that Forest might be relegated. That was harsh because I had not played in many of the matches, but there was worse to come on Monday when Matt Gillies called me into the manager's office. He came straight to the point: 'I think it would be advisable for you to look for a new club.' And I always say that Peter Shilton's save caused it.

Where Bill Taylor remembers the hard times, Geoff Hurst is a walking reminder of the golden age when England won the World Cup. Yet he seemed diffident, perhaps because he joined us as manager of only a non-League club, Telford United, or perhaps because he was an England player not so long ago and didn't want to abuse the invitation back by shouting the odds. I think Geoff Hurst has a lot to give the England squad; you can ask him for advice knowing that he has done it all. His demonstrations are great, and his finishing is still excellent – even better than the finishing of Uwe Seeler, the famous German centre forward, who sometimes does demonstrations at Hamburg.

Hurst is remarkable. Timing and instinct are his assets. He knows exactly where he is in relation to the goalkeeper; he knows what has to be done. There is no dithering, no worrying about whether the keeper might move; Geoff Hurst never shifts for anybody. The Germans would say he has '*Eine Nase*', a nose for goal. It cannot be taught, you cannot train someone to score a hat-trick in a World Cup final as Geoff did in 1966.

He cannot run about as he used to do, he's a big man and huge round the thighs. But I think, crazy though it sounds, that he is still the best finisher in the England squad, even now when he is coming up to thirty-eight. His specialities were near-post goals, decoy runs and passes played off the chest – and he honed them to perfection during a thirteen-year association with Ron Greenwood at West Ham. Hurst's trophy cabinet contains forty-nine England caps, and I imagine that he feels the demo job with us is almost like having a fiftieth. Also, just as importantly, Hurst points to the security an international player can achieve by keeping his head and his good name. There is that big Mercedes, the partnership in two booming pub-restaurants, the insurance interests, a country home with four acres and a tennis court and now the break into big-time management as assistant to Danny Blanchflower at Chelsea.

Hurst is a modern; he springs from a different world than Les Cocker who partnered Don Revie and before that worked for England with Sir Alf Ramsey. Les was a real, old-time football man from the small clubs in the middle fifties. Alan Ball once cracked unkindly, 'Les never saw a Continental until he was sixty' – but I enjoyed Les. He was good, the perfect foil for Revie, and he surprised all of us when taking charge for our match in Brazil. He picked the team and was decisive about it, saying, 'We'll play this way,' and running through the tactics. I was amazed, having always thought of him in the subservient role. For the first time I wondered if he might not have made a good number one somewhere.

The League is full of Les Cockers, gnarled men who are steeped in football but never fulfil their maximum potential because they haven't got the chat. I noticed that with Les; he knew his stuff better than most modern coaches but could not put it over as clearly. As players, he liked the workers, the ones who gave everything. They were Cocker men. We used to play games with him in practice matches. We used to kick him, he was so frail. No one was chopped down more than Les, and no one took it in better part. He could always tell a joke against himself, and none funnier than the story of his scarred lip.

It happened when he was a centre forward for Stockport County – obviously, a busy, buzzing centre forward active with the elbows because he wasn't big enough to shove anyone out of the way. The match was at Mansfield and an opposing forward was George Antonio, who had spent ten years at Stoke City playing inside right to Sir Stanley Matthews. Les gave him the verbals, 'Antonio the ice-cream cart. Ice-cream man.' And so on. Then the lights went out on Les. He used to tell us: 'I never saw what hit me. I came round in the dressing room with my face like a balloon and my lip needing stitches. When our bus left, I was sitting by a window feeling sorry for myself when George Antonio walked out of the ground, stopped opposite me and, never saying a word, licked an imaginary ice-cream.'

George Antonio lives in Shropshire now and still plays football – at sixty-three – for Oswestry School. 'The rest of the team are between seventeen and thirteen,' he says, 'but I can stick out a game as good as any of them.' He, too, still loves to tell the tale of Les Cocker's scar and gladly fills in the bit that his unconscious victim missed. This is what happened: 'Les had been niggling me all afternoon until, in the second half, I had the ball and could hear Les running up behind me. Quickly, I crossed the ball to the far side of the field where I knew all eyes would follow it and then I stuck my right fist out. Les ran straight into it. What a perfect knock-out!'

8 Keepers

Peter Shilton looks as if he could keep goal wearing a leopard skin, but as a boy he worried about being too small. He remembers: 'I had to do stretching exercises, hanging from the banisters while my mother pulled at my legs, and then reaching upwards, ever upwards, at a line on the wall.'

Ray Clemence wanted to be a goalscorer, not a goalkeeper, but, 'Every team I played in kept moving me further back after I started as an inside left. Skegness reserves used to play me at left back when they were short, and Scunthorpe signed me after a youth club final in which I wanted to play left half but was ordered into goal.'

Clemence and Shilton – no country in the world has a better pair. As I said once to Ron Greenwood when he played Peter after using Ray in every game, 'I don't know how you pick between them.' No one in football could provide me with a convincing reason for selecting one and not the other; it's a horrible problem for the manager. Yet the records show that Shilton, although a full international at twenty-one, has been overtaken in total appearances by Clemence, who started two years behind him.

But Liverpool took ages deciding about Ray. I believe he was watched eighteen times, the longest scrutiny in the memory of Anfield's scouts. Of course, it's normal for goalkeepers to be checked on more frequently than outfield players because of the games in which they have almost nothing to do. Once the scout sent Bill Shankly this terse report on an inactive Clemence: 'He collects a good back-pass!'

Shankly never saw Ray play until after he had signed him; he never saw me, either. The assessing of small fee players was left to the staff while Shanks concentrated on his first team. Perhaps he believed, 'Why keep a dog and bark yourself?', but he must have been aware of the technical query that lay behind Liverpool's hesitancy. 'The diagonal', the coaches called it, wondering if there might be a flaw in the unusual Clemence combination of being right-handed and left-footed.

No doubts – at least, not once he filled out – were ever heard about Peter Shilton's qualifications for goalkeeping. He was backed all the way from boyhood, particularly by his parents who even moved house to further his chances at Leicester City. Peter recalls: 'We lived over a shop on an estate and with a club nearby. The noise at closing time always woke me, so my parents found a quieter house; I was at school and training two evenings a week, so I needed undisturbed nights.'

Shilton succeeded the great Gordon Banks at Leicester, and followed him again at Stoke City after Gordon lost the sight of one eye in a car crash. Yet, contrary to legend, Shilton's tutor was not Banks of England. He was coached by George Dewis, a former centre forward on the youth staff at Leicester, of whom he says: 'For four years, he worked me solidly. If there's a man behind Peter Shilton, then it's George Dewis. Gordon Banks

A keeper doesn't always need his hands, as Peter Shilton shows here against Don Givens of Q.P.R. in 1974

Peter Shilton in a flying save

took me under his wing later, smoothing off the rough edges when I needed that extra polish.'

Though it is impossible to choose between Shilton and Clemence on match performances Shilton has the edge in training and everyday professional routine. He works so hard, striving for perfection and geeing himself up; 'Come on, wake up,' he tells himself whenever we put the ball past him. Just as Brian Clough, his manager at Nottingham Forest, won't be satisfied until he wins everything, so Shilton won't be happy until he never, ever lets a goal in. I have scored goals against him in England work-outs that no keeper on earth could have got near, but Shilton will blame himself, and believe he is the one man in history who should have been able to stop that ball.

I am not being unkind in saying that nature intended Peter Shilton to be a thickset lad with a weight problem, so his fitness and agility are an inspiring example to young keepers of what can be achieved by determination and flat-out training.

While Shilton stays at the top by training so hard, Ray Clemence gives equally good and often better displays without driving himself into the ground; Clem relies on natural ability, positional sense and experience. The goal that Poland scored at Wembley on 17 October 1973 to put us out of the 1974 World Cup went under Shilton's body; I think Clemence would have saved that. He was rightly the number one man during the years under Don Revie, when he almost monopolized the England jersey.

Now the tables might be turning because Shilton still wants to improve while Clem – although he has just set a League record of only sixteen goals conceded in a season – may not have the old urge. There are days when he'll say, 'Right, I'm going to stop everything', and he does; but there are other days when he'll let a few in and not be annoyed – provided, of course, that they are not real blunders.

If Clem is in the bar after a match sipping a half of lager, then you know that he is satisfied with his performance. If you don't see him, then it is a sign that he feels he has played badly. He will sulk in his room for days. Ray is a good pro and makes few mistakes, but he cannot accept that occasional errors are unavoidable. In six years together with Liverpool and England, I have seen him commit only two of those blunders that entitle a team to glare at the keeper and say, 'Bloody hell!' One was that Dalglish goal, on 15 May 1976, the other was in the League against Leicester City. He leapt for a long, high ball into the middle, got a touch but lost it. As he turned to see where the ball had gone, it dropped on his head and bounced to Keith Weller, who knocked it in.

I am a good friend of Ray Clemence; I've followed him around. I went in his digs at Scunthorpe, I took over his digs at Liverpool. I love the lad and would have said, 'There is no better keeper.' Now I'm not so sure. It's a sin that one of the two has to sit on the bench, yet England are right in resisting the temptation to say, 'We'll use both of them, we'll play them in alternate matches.' That would be wrong because it's important for a team to have a regular keeper. I'm just glad it's not my job to decide who it should be. But it is my job, as an Englishman in Germany, to defend our goalkeepers from the staggering Continental view that none of them is any good.

You won't see many goalkeeping pictures to better this – Peter Shilton leans out to catch a ball at full stretch. The match was Q.P.R. v. Leicester in 1974

Opponents, but friends – Trevor Brooking gets a pat from Ray Clemence in a West Ham v. Liverpool F.A. Cup tie at Upton Park in 1976

Over the bar goes one shot thanks to high-flier Ray Clemence at Liverpool against Manchester United in 1975

I think that England is richer in goalkeepers than any country in the world; we have so many great ones that we don't know what to do with them. So I thought it was a leg-pull when German footballers started telling me: 'What's wrong with the English game is not all those high crosses, or that you don't play enough one-twos. The weakness is your goalkeepers.'

This is the general opinion in Germany, and held quite seriously. Poor Clem is a favourite butt, and every time our keeper at Hamburg makes a mess of things in training all the lads shout 'Like Clemence!' They are thinking of Rainer Bonhof's free kick that beat him at Munich on 22 February 1978 and won the match for West Germany, and of the first goal that night when he possibly got his angles wrong and it sort of flew under his hand. Especially they are thinking of Bonhof's goal for Borussia Munchengladbach in the European Cup quarter-final at Dusseldorf in 1978. Liverpool let this one in during the last few minutes. Clem started to crouch but the ball, a dipper, scooped up and hit his shoulder. It finished in the top of the net, a tremendous shot. The Germans argue: 'If the keeper had stood up and the ball went through his hands, then it must hit his chest. One of the first rules.'

I tell them, 'How dare you criticize English goalkeepers when you have so many clowns here in long shorts and big gloves?' The Germans have Sepp Maier and two or three other very good goalkeepers. You can forget the rest. They don't know how to hold a ball, they punch everything out. Shoot straight from twenty yards and they will punch it right back to you. I wouldn't even call them goalkeepers, they are shot-stoppers. A goalkeeper is someone who commands the penalty area and catches crosses, not someone glued to the goalline who never advances further than the penalty spot.

It didn't help my case, though, when we were stuck in a Norway clubhouse for a few hours waiting for a boat during a summer tour. To pass the time, some videotapes of English games were shown – and, of course, it was all highlights of goals flashing in. And the Germans were falling about laughing as Mervyn Day of West Ham, for one, let in a few. 'Ho, ho, a typical English goalkeeper,' they kept saying. But if you showed a series of scoring highlights from any League on earth, it's inevitable that you would see some goalkeeping errors. I think the German view has been coloured – or, rather, distorted – by what they see on television.

I still believe that the weaknesses of Ray Clemence and Peter Shilton would not fill the back of a postage stamp. I keep telling the Hamburg lads, 'When I see a goalkeeper in the Bundesliga better than Ray Clemence, I'll let you know.' And I haven't yet!

Continued on page 97.

I celebrate my goal against Brazil at Wembley in 1978, and Peter Barnes joins in

Left: Close-marked in Copenhagen during the 1978 European championship tie, but I am still signalling at a throw-in: 'Give me the ball'

Above: Fabio Capello challenges Trevor Brooking in Rome during the World Cup tie in 1976, but the ball is slipped to Dave Watson

Below: John Phillips of Wales dives and gathers the ball at Cardiff in the home international series of 1974

Left: Cinderella's castle at Disneyland, Los Angeles, provides an unusual backcloth for some fun on the west coast leg of England's 1976 American tour

Above: Congratulations to scorer Stan Bowles, who turns to receive acclaim for popping England's first goal past the stricken Welsh in Cardiff in 1974

Above: Romeo Benetti, the hard man of Italy, is thanked by team-manager Enzo Bearzot for his impressive part in England's 1976 defeat in Rome

Below: Hungary's goalkeeper Sandor Gujdar sprawls for the ball at Wembley as I stick out a leg in a 1978 friendly, won 4-1 by England

Right: Daniel Passarella leads out Argentina and England file behind me at the intimidating Boca Juniors stadium in Buenos Aires, 1977

GO para Taccoui
AMARGO OBRERO
APERITIVO
AMARGO OBRERO
NARAN
THOMPSON

Left: Duel in the air at Wembley in 1977 between myself and
Johan Neeskens of Holland. England was defeated 0–2.
Neeskens was wasted in marking me. We were never going
to score, and almost prayed for an early finish

Above: Italy's captain Giacinto Facchetti is left trailing in
the World Cup tie at Wembley in 1977 when England
won 2–0

Above: Wembley 1979, the European championship tie against Northern Ireland – I am flying over keeper Pat Jennings

Below: While suspended by the West German F.A. I played for England at Munich in 1978

Right: The basis of my game is work-rate. This full-tilt run against Holland at Wembley in 1977 shows what 'work-rate' means

Left: Man-to-man marking at Munich's Olympic Stadium in 1978. England led in this friendly from the 43rd minute, only to be beaten by a late free-kick from Rainer Bonhof

Above: Jumping for joy on a frosty night at Wembley in 1978 as England, somewhat outplayed in the first half, win a friendly against Czechoslovakia, the European champions. The scorer was Steve Coppell – his first goal for England against a foreign international team

Above: England were one-down from the 10th minute against Brazil at Wembley in 1978, but saved the match with this free-kick

Below: Juggling the ball before turning against Denmark's defence during England's 4–3 win in Copenhagen in 1978

Right: Johan Cruyff, the fastest man in football, seen here on the ball for Holland at Wembley during their 1977 win

Dino Zoff, hailed in Italy as the world's No. 1 goalkeeper, rises above everyone to catch an England cross in Rome, 1976

9 Players

England will never find another captain with the poise of Bobby Moore. Everything felt right when Moore led us into the tunnel; he looked the part, he could play, he was unflappable, and it was plain that he and Sir Alf Ramsey understood each other almost telepathically. What a shame that Moore is not a millionaire now, sitting back and enjoying everything he put into football. The first time we met, he went out of his way to be kind, saying, 'You're young, don't make my mistakes', and going on to warn me about ill-fated business ventures, the fine print in contracts, and the leeches always trying to fasten on to new stars.

Emlyn Hughes, Alan Ball, Gerry Francis and myself all had fairly long runs as captain after Bobby. Each of us had faults, and it was possible to argue about our ability. There was no argument about Moore's fitness to carry out the ball; you just felt glad he was on your side.

When the team played cards, Bobby would be around watching. He never played himself, and yet, without stepping out of the background, he kept you aware of his presence. He was not the sort to bark orders like, 'I'm the skipper, so do as I say. Everything comes from me.' Bobby preferred to sit back and let things happen until intervention was needed, then he would say something sensible before melting into the background again.

There's a risk of error in offering deep opinions about footballers with whom you have played only a couple of games; even so, I feel there might be some truth in the inside stories that Bobby was a restless sleeper, a worrier and a suspected ulcer case. He could be the type to bottle up his troubles – unlike me, a spontaneous erupter at irregular intervals.

Whatever his anxieties, he never stepped on to a pitch looking less than a million dollars. Mr Perfect, that's how I saw Bobby Moore – but I don't know what label to pin on the player who ought to have walked into the England No. 6 shirt when Moore bowed out, and who ought still to be wearing it today, Colin Todd. It's scandalous that Todd has played hardly more than two dozen full games for England. But perhaps he is to blame; he could have been more ambitious. That also applies to another contender for Moore's old position alongside the centre half, because Kevin Beattie has every attribute required by a defender. He has the physique, the skill and the stamina, but there is a question mark against his attitude.

The higher you climb in football, the fewer faults you can afford to have. The Todds and Beatties never realize this because they lack dedication; I don't mean that they are not good professionals, only that they don't burn to be winners. Defenders of half their ability have more caps. Todd and Beattie are aware of this but don't seem to care. They represent those easy-going players who, I sometimes feel, would turn down an international cap for a game of darts. What England needs are more hungry fighters like Dave Watson; over thirty, but still eager because he started late and the game laid out no red carpets for him.

Watson didn't turn professional until he was twenty, which is ancient these days. 'Smallness held me back,' he explains. 'I was only 5 ft 1 in when I left school; also I hadn't any confidence and I'm the sort who dreads trials and tests. But for losing my job as an apprentice electrician through redundancy, I might never have come into football. However, as I was playing for fun three times a week I thought about trying to make a living from it and answered an invitation from Notts County.' Four different centre forwards were hurled against Dave in that trial, and none got a kick. So he was signed and launched on a trail that led to a famous F.A. Cup final victory with Sunderland and piles of England caps with Manchester City.

Bobby Moore leads out England against Portugal at Wembley in 1969

My first reaction to Watson as an international was: 'Put a ball in the air and he'll head it 100 yards, but he's not clever on the floor.' Now I consider him the most improved defender in England because he has worked so hard on his skills. He has retained strength in the air while adding quickness on the ground to a better anticipation which, as he points out, owes plenty to the experience of a couple of seasons playing centre forward.

Watson is a late developer. He must have been twenty-seven before becoming the established England centre half, but he is so fit and determined that he should have no problems in staying at the top until he is thirty-five or even a little older. In training matches, we say, 'Get Dave Watson on our side, and they can have the next two picks.' We reckon him worth two men because even in a five-a-side friendly on the eve of an international he'll want to win every ball.

Dave stripped looks as if he is breathing in; there's no stomach on him, just rippling muscle round a hollow. He's a winner who doesn't say a lot, but he doesn't miss much, either. I like him as a bloke as well as a team-mate, and I know him well because we've roomed together – which is not unlike living in a disco.

He is deep into rock, like the Status Quo group, and likes mixing with pop people. Dave's luggage must be nearly as heavy as the rest of England's baggage together, for he carries a huge, specially designed case for his cassettes, speakers and turntable. After a day or two with Dave, you go to sleep rocking. I think Bob Latchford, more of a pop fan than myself, is his room-mate now.

It's a problem when first joining a squad. The trainer says, 'You're with so and so', who may be a player you have never met before. You know none of his habits: you don't know if he pulls the chain, if he leaves the window wide open or likes it shut, if he is going to be pacing the room at dawn or still lying in bed at nine.

Rooming is part of football and stops squads from becoming cliquish, but the pairings must be done with care. Certain players are black-listed; none of us will share with them: Malcolm Macdonald, for instance. He's a popular, likeable lad until he climbs into bed, when he turns into a window-rattling snorer. Wherever England went, Supermac was always banished to a single room at the farthest end

It's beachboy Bobby Moore at Copacabana in Rio during a 1971 holiday

Bill Taylor, standing left, shouts the orders for an exercise session in 1974

With Revie (centre) and 'Supermac' Malcolm Macdonald

everywhere, we turned the chairs and table upside down, and we fixed the curtains to flap wildly out of the window. The hall-porter bustled up when we returned from training; he looked worried.

'Mr Keegan, Mr Hughes,' he began. 'Something terrible has happened. Your room has been ransacked. Would you mind going to see if any money has been taken?'

He couldn't understand why we doubled up laughing, saying, 'It's all right, don't worry.'

My wife Jean spends her life tidying up after me, but if England give me a neat, methodical room-mate then I try to be neat, too. Sometimes, even when sharing with Emlyn, I am afflicted by yearnings for tidiness and rush around putting everything into place, muttering meanwhile, 'I can't stand this mess any more.'

It's important to feel comfortable and relaxed with a room-mate, and there are nearly always one or two players in any team who don't particularly like each other. I prefer rooming with another non-smoker but attitude is more important. I look for someone who shares my belief that footballers have a duty to be helpful and polite to supporters, and should never refuse reasonable requests for autographs.

You build a lasting relationship with a regular room-mate, as I did with Mick Channon. 'You need a lackey,' I would tell him every time he lay in bed, saying, 'Go down and collect the kit, Kev, while I sort out a few winners from the *Sporting Life*.' I never normally bet but I started going halves on the horses when Mick was in the team. His interest was infectious.

Mick Channon is my favourite footballer because he is something of a rarity, a gifted player who refuses to take himself or the game too seriously. You could talk to him for an hour and be fairly sure that he would not mention football once. I know him so well that I found his life story a scream; parts of it read like the autobiography of a jockey. One chapter was entitled 'My Sporting Hero', or words to that effect; you might expect the subject to be Bobby Charlton or Pele or some other immortal whom Mick had played with or against. No fear! Mick's hero was Lester Piggott. I love Mick Channon; I have never felt closer to a team-mate, but you have to accept him the way he is. He won't change for anyone. There was a void when he left.

of the hotel. Gordon Hill was another who no one particularly wanted to share with. A cheerful lad, he had the defect of apparently being unable to stop talking. It would be chatter, chatter into the small hours when everyone else wanted to sleep.

I shared with Mick Channon for years, and then with Emlyn Hughes. We were all the same, scruffy! We would come in, change and leave our clothes lying on the floor until we put them on again. Nothing was ever hung up. Emlyn and I once shared in London at White's Hotel, near the F.A. offices in Lancaster Gate. We arrived in a mischievous mood. 'This room is too tidy,' we agreed, so we untidied it. Clothes and cases were scattered

It's a couple of years since we last played together for England but still I sometimes sit in my room thinking, 'I wish Mick were here; we'd be in Hector Macdonald's this afternoon.'

My dad backed the horses for most of his life and my mum was always on to me: 'When you go from here, leave the gambling alone. It's a mug's game.' I never forgot her advice, which is why I felt uneasy, even guilty and furtive, the first time I went with Mick to Hector's. I hoped no one had spotted me entering a betting shop. In the end, I looked forward to these little excursions from our headquarters at the West Lodge Park hotel. We would go in joking that Hector had switched his holidays from Butlins to Bermuda the moment he heard that England had picked us again. But we had some good wins as well.

Channon's gambling, though, is a hobby, not an obsession. He is not like Stan Bowles, who will finish with next to nothing – as everyone, including himself, knows. It's a shame about Bowles. So much ability and yet only five international caps. His touch is marvellous; he can trap, deflect and play off his body, and dribble through defences from the most dangerous angles. He ought to have been a name in Europe; instead, he may be remembered only as the butt of a famous crack by Ernie Tagg, his old manager at Crewe Alexandra, who sighed one day: 'Ah, if only Stan could pass a betting shop the way he passes a ball.' Bowles and I were playing partners in four England matches.

There was a spell when someone different was alongside me in almost every match. Three stand out in my mind, though: Malcolm Macdonald,

We're on our way from Heathrow – Ray Clemence (left), Mick Channon and me

Frank Worthington and Trevor Francis. Supermac scored six goals in fourteen appearances for England, but five of those goals were in one night against Cyprus. That game put Macdonald in the record books, possibly for ever, as the highest individual scorer at Wembley. It was Macdonald 5, Cyprus 0. He knocked me out of the way for one of them; I was set to score when he barged me aside and headed in. He was in the mood to score twenty if he could and yet, strangely, the match that made him also finished him. He never recovered his touch, never scored again for England.

I like Macdonald, an honest lad – perhaps too straight sometimes, for he'll say things without thinking. But as a partner he was difficult for me; I was never sure what to do. If he got the ball on his left foot within forty yards of goal, then he was determined to shoot. But my game springs to life much closer in; I like to thread through the defence,

Trevor Francis posed for this picture showing how he is doubly engaged – as an England player and as an American star with Detroit Express

exchanging one-twos. With Supermac, that wasn't on. It was almost impossible to build a tactical relationship with him; I would part with the ball but never get it back. The partnership was one-sided, and I was cast as the set-up guy while he scored the goals. Wouldn't anyone have got fed up?

Frank Worthington was a centre forward with suggestions of greater England potential than Macdonald. Some people call him 'Elvis' because he worshipped Presley, but to the international squad Frank Worthington was always 'Roy Rogers'. That name came from his cowboy boots with silver buckles, and although he plays in a headband now his height and swagger cry out for a stetson. Frank had style and a bit of class in his left foot: if he had only scored more regularly, his England career would not have ended after a mere eight appearances.

Trevor Francis is one of the few England players with whom I have never been close. He is rather reserved and, for someone who has been playing first-team football since the age of sixteen, a shade naive. Both as a player and as a person, he needs to broaden out and fulfil himself. That million-pound transfer should help, in that it takes him away from Birmingham City, a club in danger of becoming conditioned to failure, and puts him under the mesmeric influence of Brian Clough at Nottingham Forest. And the time spent in America with Detroit Express ought also to accelerate the maturing process.

I don't think we have yet seen anything like the absolute best of Trevor Francis. England will be a barrier for him, as it was for me, but he will overcome it, he will establish himself. Truly outstanding ability is never difficult to recognize; he has it, and he's going to get better and better.

Ray Wilkins is another player who needs time because, if he can stay at the top, he is a natural for England captain. In attitude he is the nearest I have seen to Bobby Moore. He accommodates people; he has time for kids, he has time for reporters. He never says anything unkind about anybody, being less impulsive than myself.

Yet Ray has problems. He has set himself such high standards that he feels wretched after a bad game and will draw attention to his lost form by lamenting publicly, 'I can't remember my last good display.' Nerves bother him. 'I'm petrified,' he whispered as we changed side by side in the Olympic Stadium at Munich.

'So are most of them,' I said, sweeping my arm round the dressing room, 'but they don't let anyone see it. Some of them will hide it by bouncing about shouting, "Let's stuff those Jerries." They're more tense than you are. Anyway, why shouldn't you be anxious? It's natural when you're in a fairly new team playing the World Cup-holders on their own ground. The more big games you play, the easier it becomes to live through your nerves. Look at the Liverpool lads here, I'm not nervous, Emlyn's not nervous, nor is Ray Clemence or Phil Neal. In five years' time, you'll see a kid with his knees knocking like yours and you'll know how he feels. But you'll feel like I feel.'

Northerners are supposed to disdain London players as 'Southern softies'. It's not true. I've told you how I admired Bobby Moore, and of my high hopes for Ray Wilkins. Londoners both of them, as

Trevor Brooking, the star we call 'Hadleigh'

is another of my favourite England players. We call him 'Hadleigh'.

Trevor Brooking was nicknamed after the title role of the television series because he, too, is tall and utterly dignified. He is also loaded with A-levels and never swears; the worst expression likely to cross Brooking's lips is, 'Oh, scum!' This will be said in a suburban drawl that sends the lads into hysterics.

We wind him up frequently. 'Is all well on the estates, Hadleigh?' we ask, or, if he is losing at cards, 'Will this mean parting with the pater's Silver Shadow?' But a lot of respect, especially from me, lies behind the joking. I recognize Brooking as one of the few England players who could slot immediately into a German team. He thinks quickly, he plays balls into space, and I understand him. Against Italy, Denmark and Northern Ireland he put four goals on a plate for me.

Ron Greenwood even used the word 'telepathy' about the fourth goal against Ireland in the European championship in February 1979 when Brooking flipped up a short corner which I, going into a crouch, back-headed for Bob Latchford to score. And I had never headed two goals in a match before until going to Copenhagen the previous month and getting on the end of Brooking's free kicks. Yet the greatest pass so far was for the first goal against Italy at Wembley on 16 November 1977. He aimed it into an area that made me go forward, and made me score. That's his special talent, and it was nice to return the compliment a little later by knocking through a ball that gave Trevor a goal, at last, after twenty appearances for England.

Some people think he is a luxury player because he doesn't follow back too often, or pick opponents up. I think he is a luxury every team ought to afford because he creates goals and entertains and delivers the sort of pass that makes good players better. This year, five years after his debut, I feel that Trevor Brooking has come into his own as an international.

Sadly some really talented players never appear in an England team. Steve Heighway was born in Dublin but lived there for only a few days, or weeks. I forget which. He could have tried for England caps under a parentage qualification but, as he confided to me once, he feared that he might never be selected. I think that was a mistake. Instead he played for the Irish Republic.

Two characters together – Terry Mancini on the left and Frank Worthington. The keeper is Jimmy Rimmer in his Arsenal days, which dates this picture 1975

Steve Heighway airborne at Anfield in 1975

Steve Heighway was one of the most important and effective Liverpool players during those six years when we were winning everything. Not only was he England class but he was not far off being the best winger in Britain. When Ron Greenwood began his managership by capping half a dozen Anfield players how could he have left out Heighway?

I was always amused by the change in Steve after a spell away with the Irish Republic team. His normal voice is the sort of middle-of-the-road, lightly accented English usual in graduates, but after a few days with Johnny Giles and the bhoyos he somehow acquired a brogue.

That can never have happened to Terry Mancini – or 'Henry', after the bandleader, as players dubbed him. He remained an unadulterated, rhyming slang Cockney throughout more than a year as a regular Irish Republic defender. The story – and if it isn't true, then it ought to be – goes that Mancini was rushed into the understaffed Irish squad after casually mentioning to Q.P.R. team-mate Don Givens that, although born in London and with an Italian surname, his dad was from Dublin. So, after years of soldiering round small clubs like Watford and Orient with no thought of an international career, Mancini suddenly found himself at Wroclaw in Poland, lining up for the pre-match ceremonies as a representative of the Irish Republic, a country he had never visited.

' 'Ere,' he is said to have nudged Givens as the band boomed out, 'this bleeding Polish anthem don't half go on, don't it?'

'Shut up,' hushed Givens, nudging him back. 'It's our anthem.'

10 Supporters

Elton John, pop superstar, is England's most famous supporter, but even his usual outfit of gleaming, high-button boots and New York Yankees cap cannot win him the title of most colourful fan. That belongs to 67-year-old Ken Baily, who has followed us round the world wearing a scarlet tailcoat and silk topper with a Union Jack taped above the brim. And the title of most travelled, longest-serving supporter belongs unquestionably to an elderly gentleman called Robert Schrecker. He eats, sleeps and drinks England football; a glance at his face after any match tells you how we have played.

Robert's a quiet, lovely man, and we are always pleased to see Mr Baily parading with his England shield aloft, but the team's first reaction to Elton John was one of wariness.

When we heard he would travel with us to Helsinki for the World Cup tie against Finland in June 1976, I could see some of the lads thinking, 'Aye, aye, pop star. Probably brash, flash and never seen a game before.' Instead, Don Revie introduced us to this unobtrusive, very shy man who said almost apologetically, 'If you care to join me after the match, I would be delighted to buy some champagne.'

We won 4–1, and Elton took us to a disco by the hotel, ordered some drinks and sat down at the electric piano. Perhaps two dozen regular clients were inside already, Finns out for a night of listening to the house group. Suddenly, they found themselves getting two hours of Elton John live, plus vocal backing from the England team. That was the best night out in my time with England because all the players stayed together. Corks kept popping, Elton kept playing, and at the end he paid for everything. God knows what it cost him!

Elton is now one of the England family, accepted as a genuine supporter and no publicity hunter. I spent some hours talking with him in Denmark and saw that he has plenty to offer football and that he is trying to do it right as chairman of Watford, convinced that we will see them in the First Division with a 40,000, all-seated stadium. How does Elton reconcile the roles of celebrity, chairman and fan? He says:

I've always supported England, I've stood on the terraces at Wembley, so what I relish now is the sheer luck of having the privilege to travel with the team, to get behind the scenes and to soak up the international atmosphere.

I don't mix normally with First Division players, so when I meet them I'm awestruck. That party in Helsinki broke the ice; John Read, my manager, was with me so we could play the organ and electric piano. It was a good old singsong that just took off, but the scoreline – winning 4–1 away – was what made it. I've known the bad nights, too, like coming away from Rome after being hammered. I get down in the dumps when England lose.

I'd like to entertain all the time but I am conscious of being a guest, that discipline must be

The symbol of England, mascot Ken Baily

upheld, and that privileges must not be abused. However, with the permission of Mr Greenwood, I took the Under-21 players for a few drinks in Copenhagen. It was fun for me because so many were Londoners – Tommy Langley, Graham Rix, Glenn Hoddle, Steve Walford and Kenny Sansom, the boy from Palace who I think will become a big star.

As a club chairman, I can no longer scream at the referee or the opposition's hatchet-man. But with England I can have a shout. I'm a fan again, and that's the best thing to be.

And how does Mr Baily, our mascot since 1966, feel about England? The question caught him slightly out of breath; he had just come in from his daily five-mile run and was setting off for his daily, year-round swim from the beach nearest his home at Bournemouth. Baily is a retired civil servant. He is a county councillor and a governor of ten schools, and has been awarded the freedom of Bournemouth – which, I suppose, is like a decoration for bravery under bombardments of oranges in Malta, snow-balls at Munich, beer cans at Hampden Park, and leeks fashioned from lino in Wales. In Moscow, I saw him ushered into the tribune of honour and seated alongside Sir Alf Ramsey. He was full of apologies. 'Don't think I planned this,' he kept saying, while trying to find space for his shield among the bigwigs. He recalls:

The Russians gave me permission to walk round the stadium but, unknown to me, a race was being staged for pre-match entertainment. The runners were pounding up behind, with me in the middle of the track lifting my topper and displaying the shield to the crowd. An official pulled me away just in time. That's how I happened to sit beside Sir Alf Ramsey, although I have often watched matches from the England bench. And only once, out of twenty-eight countries and more than 120 matches, has there been any trouble.

It was in Sofia; I had taken up my usual position, knowing that the F.A. had requested permission for my walk, when a Bulgarian official

Above : Clowning around at Luton airport with Elton John

Right : Robert Schrecker, an England fan since the days of Sir Walter Winterbottom, Mick Channon and me in Rome

came up. He appeared to be saying, 'Start now.'
In fact, he was saying, 'Don't start at all,' but I
didn't learn that until I was halfway round, when
they arrested me!'

It's like tossing John Bull into jail; I mean, who-
ever saw a prisoner in scarlet tails, brass buttons,
patent leather shoes and a topper, with red stripes
down his trousers? Perhaps the Bulgarians mis-
understood Mr Baily's V-sign, although he says he
is always most careful to keep the palm turned
outwards.

Robert Schrecker was an old England hand years
before Mr Baily raised his shield. Robert goes back
to the days of Sir Walter Winterbottom, but his
connection with international football dates to pre-
war Prague for he was a member, and later
manager, of the Czech national youth team. He is
over seventy and, having made a fortune from
plastics, he can indulge his enthusiasm for the stage
and for football. Every year he buys season tickets
for West Ham, Arsenal, Spurs and Chelsea, and
he has travelled and stayed with England since
1961.

The extent of his acceptance was shown by the
many times he sat with Sir Alf Ramsey on the
team-coach. As supporters go, Robert is almost
unique, for he keeps his opinions to himself:

I never said anything controversial, I minded my
own business and enjoyed the football. I had
always, since leaving Czechoslovakia, followed
England, but I had never travelled with them
until being invited into the coach by Walter
Winterbottom after a 3–2 win in Rome during
the summer tour of 1961. Gerry Hitchens, who
was transferred from Aston Villa to Inter-Milan
a few months later, played that day. So did
Jimmy Greaves, and Johnny Haynes and Bobby
Charlton. From then on, I went everywhere with
England, hardly missing a match. Then, in the
summer of 1977, with my hearing getting worse, I
decided it was time to stop touring. When the
team heard they made a presentation to me in
Buenos Aires. A silver salver, inscribed with the
players' names. That was very nice.

Looking back over all those years, I think
England's greatest game was not the World Cup
final in 1966, exciting though that was. Their best
display was six months earlier when they won 2–0
in Madrid with a front three of Roger Hunt, Joe
Baker and Bobby Charlton. Bobby Charlton, in
my opinion, was England's finest player; not just
because of how he played, but because of how he
behaved. He was a gentleman.

Not until leaving the country did I realize fully
how many people are heart and soul behind the
England team. We could have stocked a baby
boutique with presents from fans when our
daughter, Laura Jane, was born in Germany last
winter. Manchester crowds shouted terrible abuse
at me when I was a Liverpool player, as did London
spectators. Now the reception is friendly wherever
I go because supporters associate me with England,
not a rival club.

Did I say everyone is friendly? Well, there are
always exceptions. In fact there is a nastiness in
some spectators that has no place in sport. For
instance, I was at the dogs in Dublin on the night
before we played the Irish Republic when a fellow
came up asking, 'Kevin Keegan?' I acknowledged
it, whereupon he said quite deliberately, 'I hope
you break your leg tomorrow.' Hope you lose, can't
wish you good luck – that sort of childish rudeness
is tolerable, but how can 'Hope you break your leg'
ever be justified?

It's the picture of a lifetime for a special England supporter
Robert Schrecker with his presentation salver and the team
at West Lodge Park, Hertfordshire, in 1978

Bobby Charlton, captain for the night, leads out England in his 100th international in 1970. The opposition are Northern Ireland at Wembley

Then there was the chef who came up to me in a London hotel, saying, 'I used to like you.' That's the way he introduced himself, 'I used to like you.' That was hardly friendly. He went on, in an unvarnished Scouse accent, 'I'm a Liverpool supporter; I've followed them all my life and I loved you when you played for them. You had everything up there that anyone could want but you had to go abroad, and you just went for money. You don't care about football, you left Liverpool just because someone gave you more money.'

I was in company and didn't want to quarrel publicly with the fellow, so I said quietly, 'If you knew me, you would realize I didn't leave just for money. Anyway, what's a Scouse like you doing down here when you miss the old place so much?'

'Oh,' he said, 'hotels in Liverpool don't pay like London hotels. I can earn thirty quid a week more here.'

'You bloody hypocrite,' I said, 'off you go. Don't start telling me about moving for money.' Yet I said it with a smile, because I'm always considerate of fans and personally answer at least sixty letters a night.

It's just a drop in the ocean, though, when you are receiving a regular 1,500 letters a week. My brother Mike is now organizing my fan club, but I

My advice to professional sportsmen: never refuse a reasonable request for an autograph, but carry a fibre-tip for signing footballs

'Sign, please' says the first Hamburg fan to bag my autograph in 1977. Peter Krohn, then Hamburg's general manager, is on the left

like to handle letters myself. I'm very conscientious about it, so there is nothing more upsetting than some reproachful mum complaining, 'Kevin Keegan has not answered my boy's request for an autograph.' The answer is that if the lad had enclosed a stamped, addressed envelope I'd have got round to it as quickly as possible, but sometimes I am swamped by the sheer volume of phone calls (reluctantly, I've now had to install an answering machine) and mail. Each of those 1,500 fans imagines he is the only one who has written. Some fans think they own me; they never understand that a player may have faults like themselves, and ordinary worries and other demands on his spare time.

I've had people coming up to say, 'Your picture is in our bedroom,' or 'We have read your autobiography five times.' It makes one realize just how important football is to them, and what influence a star can have.

HITACHI

11 Germany

I hit him flush on the jaw with a left hook and followed with a right cross that stretched him out unconscious. No need to wait for the red card; I sent myself off, walking briskly towards the tunnel and an automatic eight weeks' suspension by the West German Football Association.

Bruce Woodcock, the old British heavyweight champion, owned the pub gym where I boxed as a lad at Doncaster, but it was not professional tuition that packed such venom into the hardest punches I've ever thrown. My fists were powered by five months of frustration in Hamburg, by my difficulties in adapting to a foreign country, a strange language, a new team. On that New Year's Eve, the last day of 1977, everything boiled over – though my knock-out victim, an amateur left back called Erhard Preuss, was no innocent bystander. He deserved what he got. But if you believe, as I do, that all things are for a purpose, then the two months' suspension was a piece of luck in that it provided me with the time I needed to assess myself and to examine the causes of my problems and my reasons for going to Germany, and to persuade my teammates that I did make a worthwhile contribution to the team.

My unrest at Liverpool stemmed from the feeling that I was in a rut and playing almost from memory. I knew the entire routine at corners, free kicks, where I had to stand at throw-ins, what to do when

I had the ball, where exactly Steve Heighway or John Toshack would be when I wanted to release it. So many good players were round me that the game seemed almost easy, which it isn't, and I felt no need to improve; I was becoming stereotyped. People said of me, 'He runs and works hard in a good team'; no one praised me as an individual, for I was regarded only as part of the Liverpool machine. I was worried that people might be right, so I decided on a fresh start. Hamburg looked exactly the kind of challenge I required, but it proved bigger than I had expected.

English football develops physique, strength and stamina, it teaches players to cope with pressure of fixtures and big occasions, the game itself is of high quality and there are no pushovers. Good players from England ought to be able to perform successfully anywhere in the world, provided they can handle the off-the-field vexations. These were precisely the ones I had not foreseen.

Language was the big problem; it was so frustrating being unable to question anyone who seemed to be insulting or snubbing me; I wanted to ask, 'Why? What's wrong?', but didn't know how. As a result, I was forever turning the other cheek. House-buying was complicated by hours of paperwork and filling in forms that I didn't understand.

There were laws to observe that I had never heard of; for instance, when a blizzard swept North Germany last winter and caused chaos in Hamburg all car owners were ordered to stay off the roads. Disobedience was punishable by a £500 fine and a year's disqualification. It's the law that I must carry

This picture couldn't have been taken in an English game because our authorities refuse to permit sponsors to place their names so prominently on shirts. So this is me with Hamburg

my driving licence in the car; it's the law that, in common with all residents of West Germany, I must register myself and always carry an identity card. The first time a policeman stopped me and asked, '*Ausweis, bitte*', wanting to see the card, I didn't know what he was talking about.

A four-page letter dropped through the door one day and worried us stiff; it was crammed with figures in Deutschmarks and seemed to be an official demand for money. Jean and I worked our way through the dictionary, trying to discover what it meant; in the end, we learned it was notification of another German law: 'Sweep your pavement when it snows.'

Driving on the other side of the road is another minor problem, so is driving twenty miles a day for the English newspapers, which not only cost 75p each but are usually the Welsh editions.

Shopping was hilarious; we often came home with the wrong items because we were too embarrassed to explain that we wanted something else. We went into an electrical shop to buy a fuse but didn't know the word; we tried to explain by gestures and frequent repetition of the German for 'very small'. They fetched us a plug. '*Nein, nein*,' we said, indicating something much smaller; this time the assistant returned with a set of Christmas tree lights.

It was fun, though, and I miss the shopping now that I cannot go with Jean any more. Hamburg has become like Liverpool, I get mobbed. No one bothered me at first beyond an occasional buttonholing – 'Hello, Englander. Nice to have you here', or that sort of brief greeting. Now I'm paying the price of fame, the result of frequent T.V. appearances and of being voted 'Man of the Year' by the German players themselves.

T.V. broke down the barriers of German reserve, which are higher than ours. I'm not a drinker or a pubby person, but I missed the friendliness of English pubs. It's almost impossible to spend an hour in a pub at home without striking up a conversation or being roped into a darts school; in German pubs a stranger is often shunned. Six months is the average time it takes to win acceptance in Germany, so it can be very lonely. Our theme-song for the first fortnight might have been Cole Porter's classic, 'Down in the depths on the 90th floor' – except, in our case, it was the twenty-fifth floor.

Above: Jean and I out for a stroll near Hamburg with our old English sheepdogs, Oliver and Heidi

Left: Me and the missus. I daren't hug too hard because Jean was only a few weeks away from having our first baby, Laura Jane, in the winter of 1978

After being bundled over the touchline in Frankfurt in 1978

The club put us in a room, probably costing more than £60 a night, in the Hamburg Plaza hotel with our old English sheepdogs, Oliver and Heidi. There was no place to walk them; besides, Heidi was still a puppy and not house-trained. Whenever they needed to go out we had to dash for the lift. Often we were too late. Because of the dogs, my contract stipulated accommodation in a house with a large garden, not near the top of a skyscraper. As I was new at the club, though, I didn't want to start raising objections.

House prices were our next shock. I had sold what most people would regard as a mansion for just under £40,000 so I started looking round confidently for something in that price range. 'We don't build houses for £40,000 here,' they said. 'That kind of money would hardly buy you a garage.' A decent house can still be bought for £15,000 in parts of northern England; in Germany, the double-glazing would cost more than £15,000.

My first home at Hamburg was a substantial bungalow on a nice country estate mainly of 'fertig' houses, which means assembled from a factory kit. They sell for about £80,000 and are regarded as ordinary middle-class dwellings. Swimming pools, saunas and cellar bars are reckoned as basic amenities by well-to-do Germans, but Jean and I agreed that we didn't need any of those trimmings, nor a big house. We try to be sensible, living well below our income, although, for the sake of a larger garden, we moved later to a £170,000 house. Still not a palace, by German standards.

English magazines and books (I've become a biography bookworm lately) are plentiful in Hamburg. Everything English seems to be obtainable, as was underlined for me after I mentioned in a German newspaper that I was unable to find my favourite cereal. Now I have a cupboard bursting with gift packets of Shredded Wheat from fans, and the addresses of the stockists. T.V. in English isn't available, though. That's the sort of detail a player and his family might overlook in the initial excitement of moving to Germany. But as I was never a television addict, I don't miss the programmes, and what I watch now, like films and the news, I use to help me with my German.

It's impossible to play with full effectiveness unless all the team can communicate. Shouts on the field, like 'Watch your back', are essential; I learned them parrot-fashion in three months. Technical terms used in team-talks I memorized in the same way; I had the speech without any spelling.

I picked up German as a child absorbs his native language; I listened and I imitated. My best teachers were companions in card schools for two marks a game, about 50p. Jean has A-level German, but she says I have not only caught her up, but overtaken her. That's purely the result of mixing and talking with people daily. I find the Germans considerate; they speak slowly and use simple words, and they have taken to me for going on T.V. and trying to speak their language, not caring whether anyone might laugh. Not that I think many would laugh; on the contrary, they seem to appreciate my efforts. My bad German opens more doors than would Oxford English.

Other internationals will follow me from the English League; my success at Hamburg guarantees it. In fact, several Bundesliga clubs have asked if I could recommend Liam Brady of Arsenal and the Irish Republic. I tell them, 'No.' I wouldn't want the blame if something went wrong, for the recommendation required is not a straightforward endorsement of skill. If it were only a matter of skill, then I could recommend Liam Brady with safety for I have no doubts about his ability. The problem is that I don't know him well enough to assess his character, for a player moving into a foreign country needs strong character more than talent. I found that out during my first five months in Hamburg; they were diabolical.

The other players shunned me, and there was jealousy over money – naturally enough, for I had arrived as a £500,000 signing and almost doubled the German transfer record. I imagine they also resented me as an unnecessary luxury; Hamburg had just won the European Cupwinners' Cup and the players probably thought, 'We're a good team already, so what do we need Keegan for?' Matters were made worse by some foolish pronouncements from Dr Peter Krohn, the man who signed me. He was Hamburg's business manager and brilliant at the job, but he had no idea how to set about persuading the other players to accept me. His line ought to have been, 'Our great team will be even better with this international from England.' Instead, he declared before one of the toughest away fixtures in the Bundesliga, 'With God and Kevin Keegan, we will win in Duisburg.' We lost 5-2.

Team-talks were comical because Rudi Gutendorf, the coach and a good friend to me, conducted them in three languages: in German, of course, then in English for me, and, finally, in French for our Yugoslavian, Ivan Buljan. I often heard Rudi doing multi-lingual shouts from the dugout – 'Very nice' to me, 'Très bien' to Ivan – but he wasn't a successful coach and lasted only for four months.

Krohn left as well, and the rumour spread that Hamburg would unload me, too, if they could get their money back. The view seemed to be: 'We have spent £500,000 only to get poor results; Keegan hasn't fitted in, although he's playing all right.' I have never been one for carting my football worries home, but it was unavoidable in a strange country without a close friend. Jean heard all my laments: 'I'm like a motherless child; everyone who I know has gone, and the team are still not talking to me.' And then everything blew up in that New Year's Eve match, just a friendly visit to the amateur club of Lubeck, an ancient Hanseatic town about forty miles from Hamburg.

A bouquet of flowers was presented to me for coming second to Allan Simonsen of Denmark in the European Footballer of the Year poll. The little stadium was full, and I looked forward to playing. I was punched on the chin by Erhard Preuss in my first run. He smirked and picked me up and I thought, 'I've known days like this all over the world when idiots have tried to upset me. I can cope, though; no way will this fellow make me lose my head.'

Berti Vogts of West Germany; he would always get in my team

'Then I started a diagonal run off the ball but my legs were chopped from under me. The referee didn't see the foul because he was following the ball; our trainer saw it and signalled, 'Stay down', so I lay there, telling myself to keep calm. I still hadn't even touched the ball when Preuss got me again in the fourth minute. He stuck his shoulder into my chest, leaving me doubled up and winded. The referee awarded a free kick but said nothing to Preuss, although he deserved a yellow card or, at least, a warning.

'That's the third time already,' I said to the referee in my bit of German.

'Don't tell me how to handle a match,' he snapped, so I knew he wouldn't be a lot of help.

The next incident was a long ball up the middle in the sixth minute; I dummied past Preuss but he hit me again. I jumped up and punched him twice; I thought I had killed him.

A friend from England was in the crowd. I had left a ticket for him but he spoke no German and was unable to make the man at the gate understand. So he paid six marks, just over £1.50, to stand with the Lubeck supporters. But no sooner had he pushed through to the front than he was scrambling to get out again. Only eight minutes after kick-off the two of us were in a taxi heading home. The fare was £40, and I had paid off the driver before I realized that we were locked out on a freezing afternoon. I had forgotten in the drama that our wives were shopping in Lubeck and had arranged to pick us up after the game. Jean had the house keys, and the place was steel-shuttered and burglarproof. That crowned a disastrous day.

Football discipline in West Germany is strict. Dismissal for striking an opponent carries a mandatory suspension of two months even for a first offender, which I was as far as the German F.A. were concerned.

The ban turned out to be the best thing that could have happened, though, because the Hamburg team began having fresh thoughts about me during my absence. They lost seven matches without me, three of those at home. They tumbled down the table after being in fifth place with me. The newspapers agreed, 'Hamburg may not be as good as they hoped with Keegan, but they are much worse without him.' The players began to realize that I had been an asset and that, although the team had yet to click, some games had been won because of my contribution.

It was the ultimate in happy endings when we won the Bundesliga in 1979, Hamburg's first championship for nineteen years. I was top-scorer with seventeen goals, an amazing haul for a midfielder, but it was no one-man show. A Liverpool pattern emerged. No one scored prolifically, but everyone from front to back chipped in with a few goals.

The dressing room coolness was replaced by warmth and friendship. I have never known such a transformation. Team-mates were scanning advertisements for me, trying to find bargains. One of them said he had a friend who would get cheap meat for my dogs. Soon the very players who had snubbed me originally were urging me to stay with Hamburg another season. Now I feel closer to the Hamburg players than I did to the Liverpool lads. Perhaps it is partly because we spend so much time together in training camps, but it is also because there are so many genuine guys behind that German reserve.

A suspended player is normally forbidden to appear in anything except private practice games, but England picked me for a full international towards the end of my ban. It was against West Germany at Munich on 22 January 1978. I was particularly keen to play and everyone else was happy. The Germans wanted to face our strongest line-up, and Hamburg were eager for me to fit in a game.

Out for a training run with Hamburg with Branko Zebec leading. He's the team boss who sentenced us to 100 sprint circuits of the pitch

Bernd Holzenbein of West Germany looks surprised as I make a point during the 1978 international in Munich

A blizzard swept Munich two nights before the match; the snow lay more than three feet deep in the Olympic Stadium but the pitch was cleared and rolled, so the match was on. The surface was good enough and the crowd was a sell-out. The only notable absentee was Helmut Schoen, Germany's national manager, who had flu and watched on T.V. at the training camp.

I was delighted with my performance after nearly seven weeks out of action, although the lack of match practice caught up with me in the eighty-fifth minute. Both legs went at once, and I had to go off. I would have lasted the distance, though, if my direct opponent had not been Rainer Bonhof, who is among the finest of the new dual-purpose midfielders. He marks fairly tight, but runs everywhere when Germany attack. It was my job to run back with him; the pair of us must have felt that we had covered 500 miles that night. It was suicide for me.

Stuart Pearson gave us the lead with a header that spun off Sepp Maier's left-hand post. Ronnie Worm, the substitute, equalized to inspire some joke headlines – for example, 'Worm gets Germany off the hook' – and to put himself in the record books as the first player to score against England teams on successive nights. Only the previous evening at Augsburg, centre forward Worm scored against our 'B' side and then became a late replacement in the senior squad when Schoen's flu knocked out some of the forwards.

The score was still 1–1 when I went off, but about a minute later we were beaten by a typically crafty free kick from Bonhof. He is a master at seizing every permissible advantage. He can bend the ball, and bend the law as well by persuading referees to let him steal a yard or two. Bonhof starts the ref thinking, 'If that foul had only been a bit further up, I'd have been awarding a penalty. So where's the harm?' He practises for hours, curling balls round dummy walls with his right foot. So there was no boasting, just a statement of plain fact, when he said afterwards: 'England's wall was wrong. I heard Clemence shouting to Mills, "Go wider", which he did. Then Mills was pulled back, leaving a gap two balls wide. That was enough for me, it was a professional job.'

Sir Alf Ramsey always reminded his players for

months about any free kick scored against England; he was always stressing 'That's the time when you are supposed to be organized and in control of the situation.'

Similar inquests at Ron Greenwood's camp probed into Bonhof's winner. Don Howe said, 'He was remarkably patient. At home, players would have been shouting at him to hurry up but it was almost as though he was waiting for a mistake.' The mistake was the pulling back of Mick Mills, which was particularly annoying after Ray Clemence had checked the wall three times, and after we had been practising shutting off the near post by putting an extra man on the end of the wall.

I have seen the action replay a number of times on German T.V. Bonhof bent the ball, and it then hit Mick Mills on the leg. The film shows Clemence telling Mills to go wide and then the rest of the wall pulling him back. Bonhof shot at precisely that instant. That is typical of his technique. He'll crouch on the ball at free kicks so that the keeper cannot see him through the wall, and it's a problem for the keeper if he is unsure of the kicker's exact position. Or he'll stand up so that the keeper can see him and then, just before taking the kick, stoop and shift the ball to one side. He'll watch a goal keeper checking his wall and then, without waiting for the referee's signal, shoot into the other corner. Sometimes referees order a re-take but often they don't because of their feeling that every advantage should be given to the side which has been fouled.

Peter Shilton talked about walls at Munich and the various unorthodox ideas for lining them up. He said:

There's only one way to set a wall, and that is to cover the near post by a man or three-quarters of a man's width. Your biggest man should be on the end of the wall to stop the kick going over him or to compel a high trajectory. For the same reason, walls always try to site themselves nine yards from the kick, instead of ten. It forces the kick higher. I always stand a short distance from the far post, offering that to shoot at.

You shouldn't be beaten by free kicks but it happens if there is a fantastic shot, or when something goes wrong.

Fantastic shots are common enough in Germany because Bundesliga dead-ball experts are not frightened of experiments. English players start worrying, 'What if I hit the wall, or balloon it over?'

England free kicks became as complicated as Busby Berkeley dance routines in Don Revie's days. We had players doing dummy runs in all directions, someone picking his nose there while someone else jumped over the ball here. These deep plots were often scotched quite accidentally by some idiot opponent not reacting to our diversionary tactics. By standing in the wrong position, he would ruin our free kick. Now, under Ron Greenwood, we are back to the dead simple free kick. Anywhere around the box, we have a shot. It can go in direct, it can hit someone and be deflected in, it can hit someone and rebound to us. When there is a marksman like Tony Currie in our side, the straightforward method pays best: 'Find a gap, and shoot through it.'

'Congratulations', they said at Hamburg. 'You have just been elected European Footballer of the Year. Now here's your shovel, get out and clear the terraces'

Rainer Bonhof of West Germany, perhaps Europe's most outstanding dead-ball expert

Ray Wilkins pursued by the Germans at Munich in 1978
I think Wilkins can captain England some day

The players themselves talked to Ron Greenwood about making these changes in our set-pieces. He is a manager who likes to hear our opinions; he never fails to ask me, 'What do you do in Germany that we don't do?' I told him the national team took a whole week off just to prepare for a match in Malta; League games were cancelled. They had another week together in a training camp at the end of last season; if they reach the European championship finals in Italy, the team will have a full three weeks of preparation. They not only take a chef with the West German team, they take their own food as well. They argue, 'You might just get unlucky on tainted fish, you lose your best player with food poisoning, and you lose the game.'

Club training in Germany is different than in England, starting earlier and being two sessions a day, instead of morning only. If I'm not at the training ground by half-eight in the morning and out changed within ten minutes, then I'm not allowed into the warm-up circle – which is a good game of six against two that the Germans play. So the players are out training twenty minutes earlier than they need be every day, whereas at Liverpool, although training was supposed to start at ten o'clock, we used to stroll in at ten past knowing the bus never left for the training ground until 10.15.

Once at Hamburg, I genuinely misheard the time for training. I thought it was ten o'clock and was in a full thirty-five minutes early. In fact, it was a nine o'clock start and the club fined me £125. That is standard in Germany, any lateness is fined heavily – but the fines go into a kitty for an end-of-season dinner, so I may get my money back in rump steak.

Another difference in Germany is the number of foreign coaches; there are none in England. All sorts of nationalities work in the Bundesliga; our coach at Hamburg is a Yugoslav, Branko Zebec. He played as outside left in FIFA's Rest of the World team that drew 4–4 with England at Wembley in 1953, and many people regard him as among the greatest of Yugoslavia's internationals. He has been in Germany for about twenty years but his grasp of the language is not much better than mine; I understand him well because he constructs his sentences in the way that I do, not always correct grammatically but easy to follow.

Anyone inquiring about the difference between German and English club football should train for a week under Zebec. When we heard he was joining Hamburg, our masseur said, 'I've worked with him at Braunschweig and he makes the players run forty times round the track – sprint down one side, jog across behind the goal, spring down the other side. That's eighty sprints.' Our team said, 'That's impossible, players can't run like that. We won't do it if he comes here.'

Anyway, he came. The first two or three days were very light training, and then he got us. I'll never forget Zebec placing a ball carefully on the centre spot, then sitting on it. He sat for an hour and a half while we ran and ran and ran. He sent us round the track fifty times, a whole hundred sprints. I have never trained so hard.

12 The Greatest ~ My Own Selection

Apart from a World Cup winner's medal, the most exclusive England honour is a cap against the Rest of the World. Only two of these fixtures have been played in my lifetime.

I was still only a toddler in 1953 when a last-minute penalty by Sir Alf Ramsey stopped Branko Zebec and the FIFA stars from ending England's unbeaten home record a month before it fell to the 'Magical Magyars' of Hungary. I was still in short trousers when goals by Terry Paine and Jimmy Greaves beat a Rest of the World team packed with famous forwards like Di Stefano, Puskas, Kopa, Seeler and Denis Law. And I suppose I'll be in my retirement before it is England's turn for a third fixture against FIFA, so I'll play the game on paper as a variation of the Greatest XI game.

Everyone plays Greatest XIs – especially Bill Shankly. I've seen his eyes light up with the fantasy of assembling British all-time greats like Alan Morton, Tom Finney, Tommy Lawton and Peter Doherty and sending them out to toy with the opposition. Shankly's dream went like this: 'I'd sit in the stand and say to my super-team, "Don't try for half an hour; let the others play." When the other team were four up, I'd take out my handkerchief as a signal and we would knock in ten quick goals. Then I'd say, "Right, lads. That's enough. Pack it in now."'

I am going one better than my old boss in that I am choosing two teams, a World XI and, to widen my scope, a British XI. All of them are players I have faced or partnered during my England career. I am copying Bill Shankly, though, in deciding to watch from the stand. For this game, I am neither player nor manager; I am just the selector.

I'll start with the World XI goalkeeper, which means a choice between Dino Zoff of Italy and Sepp Maier of West Germany. Maier gets the vote because I've seen him more than Zoff and, though I have seen him make mistakes, I know he is a big-match player. He would rise to the occasion of Britain v. The World as he did to three European Cup finals and the World Cup final.

Maier was an important factor in Bayern Munich successfully defending the European Cup against Leeds United in 1975 and St Etienne in 1976, and his instinctive save of a volley from Johan Neeskens stopped Holland equalizing in the second half of the 1974 World Cup final. Germans say Maier has an English character, meaning that he is carefree by nature and likes a laugh. He lives up to this image by driving a Jaguar.

Maier, at first glimpse, may seem ungainly; actually, he is most athletic and good enough at tennis to win the odd game off Bjorn Borg. Cracks are appearing now in Maier's goalkeeping; after all, he is thirty-five and the new German team manager is going for younger men. But the criterion for my teams is how the players performed at their peak. They are assumed to be at their best.

Giacinto Facchetti of Italy is my overlapping left back; it was he who popularized the technique. Facchetti is a gentleman of football (although he uncharacteristically lost his temper against England in New York), one of the few Italian defenders who

The King himself, Pele, in one of his farewell matches in 1978. But those empty seats are a disgrace

Sepp Maier throwing out against Italy in the 1978 World Cup

is fair and never engages in ripping shirts and spitting. He is above that, as I would expect from real world-class players. He played in three World Cups – in England, in Mexico and in Germany – and the Italians took him to Argentina as one of the assistants to the coach, which was really a mark of respect.

I played against Facchetti when he was growing older and not running as far as in the early days when Inter-Milan ruled Europe, but he was very fit for a man over thirty: clever, a good tackler, an accurate user of the ball, and with superb positional sense. My sweeper could advance confident of Facchetti slotting in behind him.

The right back is my good friend Berti Vogts of West Germany – and I can imagine the reaction on Merseyside: 'What, that dirty devil?' Fans don't know Vogts as the players do, though; if he is hard, he is also genuine and a fine sportsman. I'll never forget Berti Vogts turning up at Liverpool's banquet in Rome in 1977 to have a drink with me. That wasn't easy to do. I like to think of myself as a sportsman but I'm not sure that I would have dropped into Borussia Munchengladbach's party if they had won the European Cup. Think about it, all the way to the biggest final of the club season and then you lose 3–1 playing poorly. After that, I wouldn't want to see any more of the winners.

Vogts close-marked me in Rome and must have bowled me over forty times. Some defenders run

away after knocking you down but Berti was always first to pick me up, saying sorry in English. For character, he is among my all-time favourites, and he would balance well with Facchetti. One full back would be elegant and inventive, the other an out-and-out defender.

Jerzy Gorgon of Poland is my centre half. 'A donkey' was Brian Clough's assessment, but I think that Gorgon copes most effectively with his technical limitations. He is a strong stopper with some skill and would balance with my sweeper, who is best partnered by a big man willing to attack the ball.

The sweeper is Franz Beckenbauer of West Germany; no other name crossed my mind for this position. I think Beckenbauer is unique, even greater in his position than Bobby Moore. He advanced further and more often than Bobby; he made and scored more goals. Don Revie told me to mark Beckenbauer at Wembley when we beat the Germans 2–0 in March 1975. You may be thinking, 'Mark a defender? That can't be hard work'. In fact, it was impossible; I said to Revie afterwards, 'I wouldn't thank you for another job like that.'

I closed down on Beckenbauer, thinking, 'No options for you now, lad, except knocking it back to your keeper.' Not Kaiser Franz! He would pause on the ball, brush it with the sole of his boot, shuffle it aside by no more than a few inches and then, suddenly, bend a kick round me. He did that to me at least eight times.

Berti Vogts of West Germany slips in the Argentina World Cup as Roberto Bettega keeps an Italian attack moving

Giant centre-half Jerzy Gorgon of Poland wins the ball against West Germany in Argentina

A radiant Franz Beckenbauer on the greatest day of his life, the day West Germany won the 1974 World Cup

I know the full repertoires of the best sweepers in England and they rarely surprise me. Beckenbauer amazed me all night. An opponent standing three yards away, even one as small as myself, blocks the vision of any normal player. Beckenbauer is not normal; he could still see, or perhaps sense, everything behind me. He would knock the ball past knowing it would find his target. He screwed one pass round two of us with such accuracy that it drew up in the path of a German forward. Even someone who had never seen a football before could have controlled that one.

I felt a failure in victory. My job was to stop Beckenbauer floating those balls around, but I couldn't do it. He is an imperturbable opponent, he trades on impatience. Cries of 'Get on with it' never disturb him. He plays the waiting game. When I dummied to challenge, he knew already that it was only a dummy. As soon as the challenge was real, he slipped the ball by. It was uncanny.

The midfield of my World XI is going to be glued together by someone who attempted to do me in in each of our two meetings. Romeo Benetti of Italy is among the fiercest markers of my time, but he is skilful too, and phenomenally strong. Every team needs a midfield marker to cut down the opposing creator. That's Benetti's job. He is also comforting

to have around should someone on the other side start dishing it out. In that way, he would be like Tommy Smith of Liverpool who quelled trouble-makers by giving a cold-eyed stare accompanied by a wagging finger. It was always enough.

Rivelino of Brazil is my other midfield man – not the sour-tempered Rivelino seen at Wembley but Rivelino the space-maker with a cannon-ball shot. I have never played against anyone with more tricks; when he steps over the ball, I half expect it to disappear. It is best to let him perform while preventing him from getting past you, for he makes fools of would-be tacklers. Like Beckenbauer, he waits for people to dive in. Make a false step, and he's away. His other speciality is the free kick. On Brazil's 1973 tour of Europe and North Africa, the Tunisian national goalkeeper broke his shoulder trying to save one. When Rivelino plays, a free kick just outside the box is nearly as good as a penalty. They whine in like left-footed shells.

I'll never forget one of his passes in Rio, it was every inch of eighty yards. I wouldn't have believed it was possible to strike a ball so hard, so far, so accurately, until I saw Rivelino do it from the edge of his penalty area. The target man was twenty yards inside England's half and starting a full diagonal sprint to get behind Dave Watson and Emlyn Hughes. Yet the ball pinpointed him, it fell in his stride. He didn't need to change direction. I was about three yards away from Rivelino and I felt the wind as the ball passed me at shoulder height. The astonishing thing is that it stayed at the same height all the way. I watched wide-eyed as it flew on and on and on; that's one of the rare times when I've felt outclassed.

My World XI will play 4-2-4 and the four forwards are Pele, Cruyff, Muller and Kempes. The team is packed with scorers. Pele and Cruyff, though, could work between midfield and attack, changing the formation to 4-4-2 should the British XI get them under the collar. There is no problem in shifting Pele around; he is so versatile that he could even keep goal in an emergency. Cruyff, too, is flexible and can pull the strings from anywhere.

What I will never forget about Johan Cruyff is a race between us when Barcelona came to Liverpool in a European match. He broke past me on the edge of their box and, as he was only a yard away, I thought, 'Right, I'm after you!' By the time we

Roberto Rivelino of Brazil poises to unleash the world's most famous left foot. A shot from the third-place final against Italy in the 1978 World Cup

Above : Pele in full flight against the Czechs in the 1970 World Cup in Mexico

Below : Johan Cruyff just getting up speed against Benfica in a European Cup semi-final in 1972

reached the halfway line, I was nearly ten yards behind and beginning to feel that I must be running backwards. Yet I was only twenty-four, four years younger than Cruyff, and as fast as I've ever been. Like Cruyff, I can run nearly as quickly with the ball as I do without it, but never as fast as he did. 'The Flying Dutchman' was an apt nickname; until you have tried to catch him it's impossible to imagine the sheer speed.

Gerd Muller of West Germany rejoices in two nicknames: '*Der Bomber*', which is self-explanatory, and '*Der Dicker*', which translates roughly as '*The Fat Man*'. Muller would play as my central striker with Mario Kempes of Argentina a bit wider and deeper on the left.

Kempes ran his heart out to win the World Cup last year at River Plate Stadium; the reaction from those efforts seems to have shown in his club form for Valencia. But I'm not picking Kempes on Spanish League performances; he is in my team as the deadliest young finisher in the world. Nor will I listen to criticism of Muller. I know he usually looks overweight, that he never runs around a lot, and that he hardly ever produces the sort of spectacular shot that brings crowds to their feet. My reply is: 'Study his goal record.' Muller scored 628 goals for Bayern Munich and West Germany. His last goal for Helmut Schoen won the World Cup, and forty-seven minutes later he retired from international football saying, in effect, 'Follow that.' I don't suppose anyone will; there's never been a scorer like the Bomber.

Luckily for my British XI, I can choose a goalkeeper held in awe even by Muller. He is Gordon Banks – 'Banks of England' to the headline writers. Muller moved this year to Fort Lauderdale Strikers in America but, before going, confided why he declined to take a penalty against England at Wembley in 1972. He said, 'It was because Banks was in goal. He was the only keeper I ever worried about; the only one with the concentration not to be unsettled by my penalty technique, which was to stand waiting until the keeper moved and then shoot for the other corner. Banks would never move. 'That's why I handed the ball to Netzer, saying, "Here, Gunter. You take it."'

It was my sad privilege to appear in the last match that Banks played with two good eyes; that was Liverpool v. Stoke City. Next afternoon, shattering

glass in a car crash on a winding road finished him for major football, although he came back to play regularly in the North American League. It was that fantastic save against Pele in the 1970 World Cup at Guadalajara which made him famous. Pele smashed a header downwards and was shouting 'Goal' as the ball bounced a few feet from the far post, but Banks was hurling himself across and flicked it over the bar with his right hand. 'Unquestionably the greatest save I have seen,' said Bobby Charlton, but I think Banks made many of almost similar class when the whole world was not watching. He was simply a great goalkeeper, and regarded everywhere as England's best in the past thirty years. In picking my team, I give Banks the vote over Ray Clemence, Peter Shilton and Pat Jennings because he proved himself in two World Cups.

Gordon Banks in 1970. There's never been a better goalkeeper in my time

England 2, U.S.S.R. 0: 8 June 1968.
In Rome: 100,000. European Nations Cup third-
  place final.
Scorers: Charlton, Hurst.
England: Banks; Wright, Labone, Moore,
  Wilson; Stiles, R. Charlton, Peters, Hunter;
  Hunt, Hurst.
Match point: England finish third, but Italy win
  the championship after a replay against
  Yugoslavia.

England 0, Rumania 0: 6 November 1968.
In Bucharest: 80,000.
England: Banks; Wright, Labone, Moore,
  Newton; Ball, R. Charlton, Mullery, Peters;
  Hunt, Hurst. Sub.: McNab (for Wright).
Match point: Poor passing, and off-form
  midfield. A match to forget.

England 1, Bulgaria 1: 11 December 1968.
At Wembley: 80,000.
Scorer: Hurst. Bulgaria: Asparoukhov.
England: West; Newton, Labone, Moore,
  McNab; Bell, Mullery, R. Charlton, Peters;
  Lee, Hurst. Sub.: Reaney (for Newton).
Match point: Memorable for Asparoukhov's
  goal, scored after running from the halfway
  line.

England 1, Rumania 1: 15 January 1969.
At Wembley: 80,000.
Scorer: J. Charlton. Rumania: Dumitrache (pen.).
England: Banks; Wright, J. Charlton, Hunter,
  McNab; Ball, R. Charlton, Stiles; Radford,
  Hunt, Hurst.
Match point: 'Bad luck, bad finishing' – Sir Alf
  Ramsey.

Jairzinho of Brazil finds a gap against Italy in the 1970 World Cup final in Mexico City. That's Pele on the right, hemmed in and wearing No. 10

England 5, France 0: 12 March 1969.
At Wembley: 85,000.
Scorers: O'Grady, Hurst 3 (2 pens.), Lee.
England: Banks; Newton, J. Charlton, Moore, Cooper; Bell, Mullery, Peters; Lee, Hurst, O'Grady.
Match point: Two milestones passed on a wet, misty night – 200 international goals at Wembley; 100 victories against Continentals.

England 3, Northern Ireland 1: 4 May 1969.
At Belfast: 23,000.
Scorers: Peters, Lee, Hurst (pen.). N. Ireland: McMordie.
England: Banks; Newton, Labone, Moore, McNab; Ball, R. Charlton, Mullery, Peters; Lee, Hurst.
Match point: Attendance halved by live T.V.

England 2, Wales 1: 7 May 1969.
At Wembley: 70,000.
Scorers: R. Charlton, Lee. Wales: R. Davies.
England: West; Newton, J. Charlton, Moore, Cooper; Ball, Bell, R. Charlton, Hunter; Lee, Astle.
Match point: Bobby Charlton back on his best form.

England 4, Scotland 1: 10 May 1969.
At Wembley: 100,000.
Scorers: Peters 2, Hurst 2 (1 pen.). Scotland: Stein.
England: Banks; Newton, Labone, Moore, Cooper; Ball, R. Charlton, Mullery, Peters; Lee, Hurst.
Match point: England win the home international championship with their best display since the World Cup final.

England 0, Mexico 0: 1 June 1969.
In Mexico City: 105,000.
England: West; Newton, Labone, Moore, Cooper; Ball, R. Charlton, Mullery, Peters; Lee, Hurst.
Match point: A safe try-out for the 1970 World Cup.

England 2, Uruguay 1: 8 June 1969.
In Montevideo: 40,000.

Scorers: Lee, Hurst. Uruguay: Cubillas.
England: Banks; Wright, Labone, Moore, Newton; Ball, Bell, Mullery, Peters; Lee, Hurst.
Match point: A last-minute victory against the only opponents that England failed to beat in the 1966 World Cup.

England 1, Brazil 2: 12 June 1969.
In Rio de Janeiro: 105,000.
Scorers: Bell. Brazil: Tostao, Jairzinho.
England: Banks; Wright, Labone, Moore, Newton; Ball, R. Charlton, Mullery, Peters; Bell, Hurst.
Match point: England ahead and Banks saves a penalty, but Brazil score twice in the final eleven minutes.

England 1, Holland 0: 5 November 1969.
In Amsterdam: 35,000.
Scorer: Bell.
England: Bonetti; Wright, J. Charlton, Moore, Hughes; Bell, R. Charlton, Mullery, Peters; Lee, Hurst. Sub.: Thompson (for Lee).
Match point: 'England are slowing down in preparation for Mexico's heat' – Georg Kessler, the Dutch national manager.

England 1, Portugal 0: 10 December 1969.
At Wembley: 100,000.
Scorer: J. Charlton.
England: Bonetti; Reaney, J. Charlton, Moore, Hughes; Ball, Bell, Mullery, R. Charlton; Lee, Astle. Sub.: Peters (for Bell).
Match points: England slowed on heavy pitch and wasted four chances; Lee missed a penalty.

England 0, Holland 0: 14 January 1970.
At Wembley: 75,000.
England: Banks; Newton, J. Charlton, Hunter, Cooper; Bell, R. Charlton, Peters; Lee, Jones, Storey-Moore. Subs.: Mullery (for Lee), Hurst (for Jones).
Match point: England slow-handclapped and booed off.

England 3, Belgium 1: 25 February 1970.
In Brussels: 28,000.
Scorers: Ball 2, Hurst. Belgium: Dockx.

England: Banks; Wright, Labone, Moore,
    Cooper; Ball, Hughes, Peters; Lee, Osgood,
    Hurst.
Match point: England overpowered the Belgians
    in a second half of mud and snow.

England 1, Wales 1: 18 April 1970.
At Ninian Park: 50,000.
Scorers: Lee. Wales: Krzywicki.
England: Banks; Wright, Labone, Moore,
    Hughes; Ball, R. Charlton, Mullery, Peters;
    Lee, Hurst.
Match point: England uncertain, and a goal down
    for thirty minutes.

England 3, Northern Ireland 1: 21 April 1970.
At Wembley: 100,000.
Scorers: Peters, Hurst, R. Charlton. Ireland:
    Best.
England: Banks; Newton, Moore, Stiles, Hughes;
    Mullery, Coates, R. Charlton, Peters; Kidd,
    Hurst. Sub.: Bell (for Newton).
Match point: Bobby Charlton's hundredth cap.
    He captained the side and was presented with a
    silver salver engraved with the flags of the
    thirty-one countries against whom he had
    played.

England 0, Scotland 0: 24 April 1970.
At Hampden Park: 137,000.
England: Banks; Newton, Labone, Moore,
    Hughes; Ball, Stiles, Peters; Thompson, Astle,
    Hurst. Sub.: Mullery (for Thompson).
Match point: First goalless draw with Scotland
    since 1872.

England 4, Colombia 0: 20 May 1970.
In Bogota: 40,000.
Scorers: Peters 2, R. Charlton, Ball.
England: Banks; Newton, Labone, Moore,
    Cooper; Ball, R. Charlton, Mullery, Peters;
    Lee, Hurst.
Match point: A ninety-second goal began this
    success at 8,600 feet.

England 2, Ecuador 0: 24 May 1970.
In Quito: 40,000.
Scorers: Lee, Kidd.
England: Banks; Newton, Labone, Moore,

Cooper; Ball, R. Charlton, Mullery, Peters;
    Lee, Hurst. Subs.: Kidd (for Lee), Sadler (for
    Charlton).
Match point: Final trial for the World Cup, and
    at 9,300 feet in the Andes. 'The players felt
    worse effects from the altitude than in Bogota'
    – Sir Alf Ramsey.

World Cup: 2 June 1970.
England 1, Rumania 0.
At Guadalajara: 40,000.
Scorer: Hurst.
England: Banks; Newton, Labone, Moore,
    Cooper; Ball, R. Charlton, Mullery, Peters;
    Lee, Hurst. Subs.: Wright (for Newton),
    Osgood (for Lee).
Match point: Solid start to England's defence of
    the World Cup, but they had to wait seventy
    minutes for the goal.

Poland's goalkeeper Jan Tomaszewski leaps to catch a
header from Colin Bell at Wembley in 1973. His display –
'The best I've seen from a visiting goalkeeper,' said Sir Alf
Ramsey – stopped England from qualifying for the World
Cup in West Germany. I was on the bench that night

World Cup: 7 June 1970.
England 0, Brazil 1.
At Guadalajara: 72,000.
Scorer (for Brazil): Jairzinho.
England: Banks; Wright, Labone, Moore, Cooper; Ball, R. Charlton, Mullery, Peters; Lee, Hurst. Subs.: Astle (for Lee), Bell (for Charlton).
Match point: Famous for the save in the tenth minute by Gordon Banks of a Pele header bouncing only a few feet from his far post.

World Cup: 11 June 1970.
England 1, Czechoslovakia 0.
At Guadalajara: 40,000.
Scorer: Clarke (pen.).
England: Banks; Newton, J. Charlton, Moore, Cooper; Bell, R. Charlton, Mullery, Peters; Astle, Clarke. Subs.: Ball (for R. Charlton), Osgood (for Astle).
Match point: Allan Clarke, in his first international, scores a controversial penalty in the forty-eighth minute.

World Cup: 14 June 1970.
England 2, West Germany 3 – after extra time. The score at ninety minutes: 2-2.
At Leon: 26,000.
Scorers: Mullery, Peters. West Germany: Beckenbauer, Seeler, Muller.
England: Bonetti; Newton, Labone, Moore, Cooper; Ball, R. Charlton, Mullery, Peters; Lee, Hurst. Subs.: Hunter (for Peters), Bell (for Charlton).
Match point: England, two-up until the sixty-ninth minute, tired in the tropical heat and went on the defensive to save energies for the semi-final three days hence. Instead, they were taken into extra time and knocked out by Gerd Muller, top-scorer with ten goals in the Mexico World Cup.

England 3, East Germany 1: 25 November 1970.
At Wembley: 93,000.
Scorers: Lee, Peters, Clarke. East Germany: Vogel.
England: Shilton; Hughes, Sadler, Moore, Cooper; Ball, Mullery, Peters, Lee; Hurst, Clarke.

Match points: A sprightly return to the 4-3-3 system on a Wembley pitch almost fully recovered from the ravages of the Horse of the Year show. The star: Francis Lee.

England 1, Malta 0: 3 February 1971.
At Gzira: 33,000. European championship.
Scorer: Peters.
England: Banks; Reaney, McFarland, Hunter, Hughes; Ball, Mullery, Harvey, Peters; Royle, Chivers.
Match point: The start of the European championship qualifying series, but England looked uninterested on a sand-pitch prepared by steam-roller!

England 3, Greece 0: 21 April 1971.
At Wembley: 55,000. European championship.
Scorers: Chivers, Hurst, Lee.
England: Banks; Storey, McFarland, Moore, Hughes; Ball, Mullery, Peters, Lee; Chivers, Hurst. Sub.: Coates (for Ball).
Match point: Slow-handclaps stilled by the strong finish of two goals in the final twenty minutes for another victory in the qualifying group.

England 5, Malta 0: 12 May 1971.
At Wembley: 41,000. European championship.
Scorers: Chivers 2, Lee, Clarke (pen.), Lawler.
England: Banks; Lawler, McFarland, Moore, Cooper; Coates, Hughes, Peters; Lee, Chivers, Clarke. Sub.: Ball (for Peters).
Match point: Gordon Banks didn't have a shot to save. He didn't even have a goal kick and he handled the ball only four times.

England 1, Northern Ireland 0: 15 May 1971.
At Belfast: 33,000.
Scorer: Clarke.
England: Banks; Madeley, McFarland, Moore, Cooper; Ball, Storey, Peters; Lee, Chivers, Clarke.
Match point: Hotly disputed winner because Francis Lee apparently handled before passing to Allan Clarke.

England 0, Wales 0: 19 May 1971.
At Wembley: 70,000.

England: Shilton; Lawler, Lloyd, Hughes,
  Cooper; Smith, Coates, Peters; Lee, Hurst,
  Brown. Sub.: Clarke (for Hurst).
Match point: Slow-handclapped and booed off.

England 3, Scotland 1: 22 May 1971.
At Wembley: 100,000.
Scorers: Peters, Chivers 2. Scotland: Curran.
England: Banks; Lawler, McFarland, Moore,
  Cooper; Ball, Storey, Peters; Lee, Chivers,
  Hurst. Sub.: Clarke (for Lee).
Match point: A brilliant first twenty minutes,
  starring Martin Chivers, clinches the home
  international championship.

England 3, Switzerland 2: 13 October 1971.
At Basle: 56,000. European championship.
Scorers: Hurst, Chivers, Wiebel (o.g.).
  Switzerland: Jeandupeux, Kuenzli.
England: Banks; Lawler, McFarland, Moore,
  Cooper; Mullery, Madeley, Peters; Lee,
  Chivers, Hurst. Sub.: Radford (for Hurst).
Match point: The Swiss faded in second half as
  England gained a fourth consecutive victory in
  the European qualifying group.

The proudest moment in a footballer's life – when the World
Cup is in his hands. Here, the happy man is Sepp Maier,
West Germany's goalkeeper. The place, of course, is
Munich after the 1974 final against Holland

England 1, Switzerland 1: 10 November 1971.
At Wembley: 100,000. European championship.
Scorers: Summerbee. Switzerland: Odermatt.
England: Shilton; Madeley, Lloyd, Moore,
  Cooper; Ball, Storey, Hughes; Summerbee,
  Hurst, Lee. Subs.: Chivers (for Summerbee),
  Marsh (for Lee).
Match point: 'I don't dare to think how many
  passes went astray' – Sir Alf Ramsey.

England 2, Greece 0: 1 December 1971.
In Athens: 45,000. European championship.
Scorers: Hurst, Chivers.
England: Banks; Madeley, McFarland, Moore,
  Hughes; Ball, Bell, Peters; Lee, Chivers,
  Hurst.
Match point: England dominated the final twenty
  minutes to reach the European quarter-finals,
  although missing five excellent chances – with
  Francis Lee twice hitting the post.

England 1, West Germany 3: 29 April 1972.
At Wembley: 100,000. European championship.
Scorers: Lee. West Germany: Hoeness, Netzer
  (pen.), Muller.
England: Banks; Madeley, Moore, Hunter,
  Hughes; Ball, Bell, Peters; Lee, Chivers,
  Hurst. Sub.: Marsh (for Hurst).
Match point: England, without a specialist centre
  half, were outplayed by the faster, younger
  Germans in this European quarter-final – a
  third consecutive victory for Helmut Schoen
  against Ramsey.

England 0, West Germany 0: 13 May 1972.
In West Berlin: 82,000. European championship.
England: Banks; Madeley, McFarland, Moore,
  Hughes; Ball, Storey, Bell, Hunter; Chivers,
  Marsh. Subs.: Summerbee (for Marsh), Peters
  (for Hunter).
Match point: A wet, depressing day with football
  to match as England, conceding twenty-seven
  serious fouls to Germany's nine, went out of
  the European championship while Helmut
  Schoen dubbed them 'Brutal'.

England 3, Wales 0: 20 May 1972.
In Cardiff: 34,000.
Scorers: Hughes, Marsh, Bell.

England: Banks; Madeley, McFarland, Moore,
    Hughes; Bell, Storey, Hunter; Summerbee,
    Macdonald, Marsh.
Match point: 'They paralysed us; we never had a
    kick,' said Terry Hennessey of Wales.

England 0, Northern Ireland 1: 23 May 1972.
At Wembley: 64,000.
Scorer (for N. Ireland): Neill.
England: Shilton; Todd, Lloyd, Hunter,
    Hughes; Bell, Storey, Currie; Summerbee,
    Macdonald, Marsh. Subs.: Peters (for Currie),
    Chivers (for Macdonald).
Match points: First game to kick off without any
    of the 1966 World Cup final side, and the first
    defeat by a British team for five years.

England 1, Scotland 0: 27 May 1972.
At Hampden Park: 119,000.
Scorer: Ball.
England: Banks; Madeley, McFarland, Moore,
    Hughes; Ball, Storey, Bell, Hunter; Chivers,
    Marsh. Sub.: Macdonald (for Marsh).
Match point: 'If this is international football, it's
    a disgrace,' said Scottish F.A. president Hugh
    Nelson after a violent match with forty-six
    serious fouls and the booking of Alan Ball and
    two Scots, Billy McNeill and Asa Hartford.

A shot from my Liverpool days, tumbling with Nick Holmes
of Southampton in the 1976 Charity Shield at Wembley

England 1, Yugoslavia 1: 11 October 1972.
At Wembley: 50,000.
Scorers: Royle. Yugoslavia: Vladic.
England: Shilton; Mills, Blockley, Moore,
    Lampard; Ball, Storey, Bell; Channon, Royle,
    Marsh.
Match point: An experimental side, with four
    new caps, fell apart after a disallowed goal and
    was almost beaten in the last ten minutes when
    Yugoslavia missed four chances.

England 1, Wales 0: 15 November 1972.
At Cardiff: 36,384. World Cup qualifier.
Scorer: Bell.
England: Clemence; Storey, McFarland, Moore,
    Hughes; Ball, Bell, Hunter; Keegan, Chivers,
    Marsh.
Match point: Kevin Keegan's debut – in a game
    that Sir Alf Ramsey called 'Neither exciting,
    nor entertaining'.

England 1, Wales 1: 24 January 1973.
At Wembley: 62,000. World Cup qualifier.
Scorers: Hunter. Wales: Toshack.
England: Clemence; Storey, McFarland, Moore,
    Hughes; Ball, Bell, Hunter; Keegan, Chivers,
    Marsh.
Match point: England had 80 per cent of the play
    but their only goal was a 25-yarder. Booed off.

England 5, Scotland 0: 14 February 1973.
At Hampden Park: 48,000. Centenary match.
Scorers: Lorimer (o.g.), Clarke 2, Channon,
    Chivers.
England: Shilton; Storey, Madeley, Moore,
    Hughes; Ball, Bell, Peters; Channon, Chivers,
    Clarke.
Match points: Bobby Moore's hundredth cap and
    Willie Ormond's debut as Scotland manager –
    and the match was as good as over after
    fourteen minutes when the Scots were 3–0
    down on an icy pitch.

England 2, Northern Ireland 1: 12 May 1973.
At Everton: 29,865.
Scorers: Chivers 2. N. Ireland: Clements (pen.).
England: Shilton; Storey, McFarland, Moore,
    Nish; Ball, Bell, Peters; Channon, Chivers,
    Richards.

Match point: Brilliant start until jolted by the
penalty; England finished to slow-handclapping
and jeers.

England 3, Wales 0: 15 May 1973.
At Wembley: 38,000.
Scorers: Chivers, Channon, Peters.
England: Shilton; Storey, McFarland, Moore,
Hughes; Ball, Bell, Peters; Channon, Chivers,
Clarke.
Match point: England's first win at Wembley
since May 1971.

England 1, Scotland 0: 19 May 1973.
At Wembley: 100,000.
Scorer: Peters.
England: Shilton; Storey, McFarland, Moore,
Hughes; Ball, Bell, Peters; Channon, Chivers,
Clarke.
Match point: Super-save by Peter Shilton from
Kenny Dalglish near the end, so England win
the home championship with maximum points.

England 1, Czechoslovakia 1: 27 May 1973.
At Sparta Stadium, Prague: 22,000.
Scorers: Clarke. Czechoslovakia: Novak.
England: Shilton; Madeley, McFarland, Moore,
Storey; Bell, Ball, Peters; Channon, Chivers,
Clarke.
Match point: A lethargic display on a bumpy
pitch; the match was saved by Clarke's 89th-
minute equalizer.

England 0, Poland 2: 6 June 1973.
At Chorzow: 100,000. World Cup qualifier.
Scorers (for Poland): Moore (o.g.), Lubanski.
England: Shilton; Madeley, McFarland, Moore,
Hughes; Ball, Bell, Storey, Peters; Chivers,
Clarke.
Match point: Alan Ball sent off in the seventy-
eighth minute after a row with Gadocha, the
Polish forward.

England 2, Russia 1: 10 June 1973.
At Lenin Stadium, Moscow: 80,000.
Scorers: Chivers, Khurtsilava (o.g.). U.S.S.R.:
Muntian (pen.).
England: Shilton; Madeley, McFarland, Moore,
Hughes; Currie, Storey, Peters; Channon,

Chivers, Clarke. Subs.: Macdonald (for
Clarke), Hunter (for Peters), Summerbee (for
Channon).
Match point: Tony Currie was impressive as
deputy for Alan Ball, suspended by FIFA from
the next World Cup match.

England 0, Italy 2: 14 June 1973.
At Turin: 60,000.
Scorers (for Italy): Anastasi, Capello.
England: Shilton; Madeley, McFarland, Moore,
Hughes; Currie, Storey, Peters; Channon,
Chivers, Clarke.
Match points: Bobby Moore's 107th cap, a world
record, and Italy's first victory against England.

England 7, Austria 0: 26 September 1973.
At Wembley: 48,000.
Scorers: Channon 2, Clarke 2, Chivers, Currie,
Bell.
England: Shilton; Madeley, McFarland, Hunter,
Hughes; Currie, Bell, Peters; Channon,
Chivers, Clarke.
Match point: 'England can still teach the world
how to play' – Austria's manager, Leopold
Stastny.

England 1, Poland 1: 17 October 1973.
At Wembley: 100,000. World Cup qualifier.
Scorers: Clarke (pen.). Poland: Domarski.
England: Shilton; Madeley, McFarland, Hunter,
Hughes; Currie, Bell, Peters; Channon,
Chivers, Clarke. Sub.: Hector (for Chivers).
Match point: Out of the World Cup! England,
even with twenty-three corners and thirty-five
goal attempts, could score only with a disputed
penalty against Poland's Jan Tomaszewski –
'I've never seen a better display by a visiting
keeper,' said Sir Alf Ramsey.

England 0, Italy 1: 14 November 1973.
At Wembley: 88,000.
Scorer (for Italy): Capello.
England: Shilton; Madeley, McFarland, Moore,
Hughes; Currie, Bell, Peters; Channon,
Osgood, Clarke. Sub.: Hector (for Clarke).
Match points: Frustrated by a typically Italian
defence and beaten in the eighty-eighth minute.
Bobby Moore's 108th, and final, cap.

England 0, Portugal 0: 3 April 1974.
In Lisbon: 20,000.
England: Parkes; Nish, Watson, Todd, Pejic;
    Dobson, Brooking, Peters; Bowles, Channon,
    Macdonald. Sub.: Ball (for Macdonald).
Match point: Six new caps, because of
    withdrawals and an F.A. Cup semi-final replay.
    This was the end of the Ramsey era; he was
    sacked three weeks later.

Joe Mercer, a director of Coventry City and a
former England player, took over for a month as
caretaker manager during these seven matches of
the home championship and summer tour.

England 2, Wales 0: 11 May 1974.
At Cardiff: 25,734.
Scorers: Bowles, Keegan.
England: Shilton; Nish, Todd, McFarland,
    Pejic; Bell, Hughes, Weller; Channon, Keegan,
    Bowles.
Match point: A bad first half-hour, then England
    began creating chances.

England 1, Northern Ireland 0: 15 May 1974.
At Wembley: 45,500.
Scorer: Weller.
England: Shilton; Nish, Todd, McFarland,
    Pejic; Bell, Hughes, Weller; Channon, Keegan,
    Bowles. Subs.: Worthington (for Bowles),
    Hunter (for McFarland).
Match points: Colin Bell the star, and Roy
    McFarland put out for six months by an
    achilles injury.

England 0, Scotland 2: 18 May 1974.
At Hampden Park: 93,271.
Scorers (for Scotland): Pejic (o.g.), Todd (o.g.).
England: Shilton; Nish, Todd, Hunter, Pejic;
    Weller, Hughes, Bell, Peters; Channon,
    Worthington. Subs.: Watson (for Hunter),
    Macdonald (for Worthington).
Match point: England's defence, without a
    specialist centre half until Dave Watson came
    on for the second half, was pulled apart by
    Scotland's Joe Jordan.

England 2, Argentina 2: 22 May 1974.
At Wembley: 68,000.
Scorers: Channon, Worthington. Argentina:
    Kempes 2 (1 pen.).
England: Shilton; Hughes, Todd, Watson,
    Lindsay; Weller, Bell, Brooking; Channon,
Keegan, Worthington.
Match point: Argentina, with their own referee,
    equalized from an 89th-minute penalty.

England 1, East Germany 1: 29 May 1974.
At Leipzig: 95,000.
Scorers: Channon. E. Germany: Streich.
England: Clemence; Hughes, Todd, Watson,
    Lindsay; Dobson, Bell, Brooking; Channon,
    Keegan, Worthington.
Match point: England hit the posts four times
    before saving the match from a free kick.

England 1, Bulgaria 0: 1 June 1974.
At Sofia: 65,000.
Scorer: Worthington.
England: Clemence; Hughes, Todd, Watson,
    Lindsay; Dobson, Bell, Brooking; Channon,
    Keegan, Worthington.
Match point: 'A fabulous performance,' said Joe
    Mercer.

England 2, Yugoslavia 2: 5 June 1974.
At Belgrade: 90,000.
Scorers: Channon, Keegan. Yugoslavia: Petkovic,
    Oblak.
England: Clemence; Hughes, Todd, Watson,
    Lindsay; Dobson, Bell, Brooking; Channon,
    Keegan, Worthington. Sub.: Macdonald (for
    Worthington).
Match point: Kevin Keegan, who had been
    beaten up on arrival by airport guards, bravely
    headed the 75th-minute equalizer.

Don Revie, manager of Leeds United and a former
England forward, was appointed full-time manager
of England in June 1974. He reigned for three years
and thirty-one matches before resigning to join the
United Arab Emirates as national manager.

England 3, Czechoslovakia 0: 30 October 1974.
At Wembley: 86,000. European championship
    qualifier.

Scorers: Channon, Bell 2.

England: Clemence; Madeley, Watson, Hunter, Hughes; Dobson, Bell, G. Francis; Keegan, Worthington, Channon. Subs.: Brooking (for Dobson), Thomas (for Worthington).

Match points: 'Land of Hope and Glory' song-sheets, a new team-strip with shoulder-stripes, and three goals in nine minutes after a double substitution.

England 0, Portugal 0: 20 November 1974.

At Wembley: 85,700. European championship qualifier.

England: Clemence; Madeley, Watson, Hughes, Cooper; Brooking, G. Francis, Bell; Channon, Clarke, Thomas. Subs.: Todd (for Cooper), Worthington (for Clarke).

Match point: Don Revie and the team were booed off after failing against Portugal's man-to-man marking, sweeper and offside trap.

England 2, West Germany 0: 12 March 1975.

At Wembley: 100,000.

Scorers: Bell, Macdonald.

England: Clemence; Whitworth, Watson, Todd, Gillard; Bell, Ball, Hudson; Keegan, Macdonald, Channon.

Match point: The first defeat of West Germany since winning the 1974 World Cup in Munich.

England 5, Cyprus 0: 16 April 1975.

At Wembley: 68,000. European championship qualifier.

Scorer: Macdonald 5.

England: Shilton; Madeley, Todd, Watson, Beattie; Bell, Ball, Hudson; Channon, Macdonald, Keegan. Sub.: Thomas (for Channon).

Match point: Malcolm Macdonald, with four headers and one left-footed shot, set an all-time Wembley scoring record and became only the fifth England scorer of five goals – after Willie Hall (1938), G. O. Smith (1899), Steve Bloomer (1896) and Howard Vaughton (1882).

England 1, Cyprus 0: 11 May 1975.

At Limassol: 21,000. European championship qualifier.

Scorer: Keegan.

England: Clemence; Whitworth, Todd, Watson, Beattie; Bell, Ball; Channon, Keegan, Macdonald, Thomas. Subs.: Hughes (for Beattie), Tueart (for Thomas).

Match point: All over in six minutes with Kevin Keegan's header from a Dave Thomas corner.

England 0, Northern Ireland 0: 17 May 1975.

At Windsor Park, Belfast: 36,500.

England: Clemence; Whitworth, Todd, Watson, Hughes; Bell, Ball, Viljoen; Keegan, Macdonald, Tueart. Sub.: Channon (for Macdonald).

Match point: England, in first visit to Belfast for four years, equalled their own record of six consecutive clean-sheets.

England 2, Wales 2: 21 May 1975.

At Wembley: 53,000.

Scorers: Johnson 2. Wales: Toshack, Griffiths.

England: Clemence; Whitworth, Todd, Watson, Gillard; Ball, Viljoen, G. Francis; Channon, Johnson, Thomas. Sub.: Little (for Channon).

Match point: David Johnson, in his debut, saved England from a first Wembley defeat by Wales with an 85th-minute equalizer.

Heads, it's in! A goal for me against Luxembourg in the World Cup qualifying group in 1977 at Wembley. It was one of five for England

England 5, Scotland 1: 24 May 1975.
At Wembley: 100,000.
Scorers: G. Francis 2, Beattie, Bell, Johnson.
    Scotland: Rioch (pen.).
England: Clemence; Whitworth, Todd, Watson,
    Beattie; Bell, Ball, G. Francis; Keegan,
    Johnson, Channon. Sub.: Thomas (for
    Keegan).
Match point: England scored twice in the first
    seven minutes of the biggest win against
    Scotland at Wembley since 1961.

England 2, Switzerland 1: 3 September 1975.
At Basle: 25,000.
Scorers: Keegan, Channon. Switzerland: Muller.
England: Clemence; Whitworth, Todd, Watson,
    Beattie; G. Francis, Currie, Bell; Channon,
    Johnson, Keegan. Sub. Macdonald (for
    Johnson).
Match point: England were two up in nineteen
    minutes, despite Kevin Keegan missing a
    penalty, but fell away in the second half.

England v. Czechoslovakia – abandoned:
    29 October 1975.
At Bratislava: 58,000. European championship
    qualifier.
England: Clemence; Madeley, Todd, McFarland,
    Gillard; Bell, G. Francis, Keegan; Channon,
    Macdonald, Clarke.
Match point: Delayed start, interrupted by fog,
    finally abandoned after seventeen minutes.

England 1, Czechoslovakia 2: 30 October 1975.
At Bratislava: 45,000. European championship
    qualifier.
Scorers: Channon. Czechoslovakia: Nehoda,
    Gallis.
England: Clemence; Madeley, Todd, McFarland,
    Gillard; Bell, G. Francis, Keegan; Channon,
    Macdonald, Clarke. Subs.: Watson (for
    McFarland), Thomas (for Channon).
Match points: England, one up after twenty-
    six minutes, beaten when Masny made two
    goals in three minutes. The Czech reserve
    goalkeeper Vencel was sent off from the
    substitutes bench in the second half for dissent.

England 1, Portugal 1: 19 November 1975.

At Sporting Lisbon: 40,000. European
    championship qualifier.
Scorers: Channon. Portugal: Rodrigues.
England: Clemence; Whitworth, Todd, Watson,
    Beattie; G. Francis, Madeley, Brooking;
    Channon, Macdonald, Keegan. Subs.: Clarke
    (for Macdonald), Thomas (for Madeley).
Match point: England, one down through a free
    kick that 'bent' four yards, equalized from a
    deflected free kick. Out of the European
    championships unless the Czechs dropped a
    point in Cyprus (which they didn't!).

England 2, Wales 1: 24 March 1976.
At Wrexham: 20,927. Centenary match.
Scorers: Kennedy, Taylor. Wales: Curtis.
England: Clemence; Cherry, Thompson, Doyle,
    Neal; Mills, Brooking, Kennedy; Channon,
    Keegan, Boyer. Subs.: Clement (for Cherry),
    Taylor (for Channon).
Match points: Kevin Keegan captain for the first
    time. Peter Taylor of Crystal Palace the first
    Third Division player for England since 1961.

England 1, Wales 0: 8 May 1976.
At Cardiff: 24,592.
Scorer: Taylor.
England: Clemence; Clement, Thompson,
    Greenhoff, Mills; G. Francis, Towers,
    Kennedy; Taylor, Pearson, Keegan.
Match point: England were outplayed in the first
    half-hour but won with a twenty-yarder as the
    Welsh hesitated, expecting a free kick.

England 4, Northern Ireland 0: 11 May 1976.
At Wembley: 50,000.
Scorers: G. Francis, Channon 2 (1 pen.), Pearson.
England: Clemence; Todd, Thompson,
    Greenhoff, Mills; Keegan, G. Francis,
    Kennedy; Channon, Pearson, Taylor. Subs.:
    Royle (for Channon), Towers (for Taylor).
Match point: Mick Channon, dropped against
    Wales, scored twice in the thirty-fifth minute.

England 1, Scotland 2: 15 May 1976.
At Hampden Park: 85,165.
Scorers: Channon. Scotland: Masson, Dalglish.
England: Clemence; Todd, Thompson,
    McFarland, Mills; Keegan, G. Francis,

Kennedy; Channon, Pearson, Taylor. Subs.:
Cherry (for Pearson), Doyle (for McFarland).
Match point: England, one up in eleven minutes,
let in a header from a corner and then the
winner through Ray Clemence's legs. So
Scotland win the home championship outright
for the first time since 1967.

England 0, Brazil 1: 23 May 1976.
At Los Angeles: 32,495. U.S. Bicentennial
tournament.
Scorer (for Brazil): Roberto.
England: Clemence; Todd, Doyle, Thompson,
Mills; G. Francis, Cherry, Brooking; Keegan,
Pearson, Channon.
Match point: Brazil, revitalized by second-half
substitute Francisco Marinho, won in the
eighty-eighth minute.

England 3, Italy 2: 28 May 1976.
At Yankee Stadium, New York: 40,650. U.S.
Bicentennial tournament.
Scorers: Channon 2, Thompson. Italy: Graziani 2.
England: Rimmer; Clement, Thompson, Doyle,
Neal; Towers, Wilkins, Brooking; Channon,
Royle, Hill. Subs.: Corrigan (for Rimmer),
Mills (for Neal).
Match point: England were two down after only
eighteen minutes of this Bicentennial match,
but won with three goals in the first seven
minutes of the second half.

England 3, Team America 1: 31 May 1976.
At Philadelphia: 16,231. Bicentennial tournament.
Scorers: Keegan 2, G. Francis. America:
Scullion.
England: Clemence; Todd, Thompson,
Greenhoff, Mills; G. Francis, Cherry,
Brooking; Keegan, Pearson, Channon. Subs.:
Taylor (for Keegan), Doyle (for Todd).
Match point: 'Not a full international,' ruled the
F.A. later, but the match is included here for
interest, especially as the opposition included
Bobby Moore, Tommy Smith and Pele, who
warned, 'England must raise individual
standards.'

England 4, Finland 1: 13 June 1976.
At Helsinki: 24,336. World Cup qualifier.

Johnny Rep of Holland beats Passarella and Gallego (No. 6)
in the air early in the 1978 World Cup final at River Plate
stadium, Buenos Aires

Scorers: Pearson, Keegan 2, Channon. Finland:
Paatelainen.
England: Clemence; Todd, Thompson, Madeley,
Mills; G. Francis, Cherry, Brooking; Channon,
Pearson, Keegan.
Match point: 'At the time we never realized what
a great result this was,' says Kevin Keegan.

England 1, Irish Republic 1: 8 September 1976.
At Wembley: 51,000.
Scorers: Pearson. Irish: Daly (pen.).
England: Clemence; Todd, McFarland,
Greenhoff, Madeley; Cherry, Wilkins,
Brooking: George, Pearson, Keegan. Sub.:
Hill (for George).
Match point: 'A collective failure,' said Don
Revie.

England 2, Finland 1: 13 October 1976.
At Wembley: 98,000. World Cup qualifier.
Scorers: Tueart, Royle. Finland: Nieminen.
England: Clemence; Todd, Thompson,
Greenhoff, Beattie; Wilkins, Brooking;
Channon, Keegan, Royle, Tueart. Subs.: Hill
(for Tueart), Mills (for Brooking).
Match point: England started with a goal in three
minutes, but finished with the crowd chanting
'Rubbish' and with Ray Clemence booked for a
professional foul.

Paddy Mulligan and me at Wembley in 1976, a night when the Irish Republic gave us something of a lesson even though we drew 1-1

England 0, Italy 2: 17 November 1976.
At Rome: 70,718. World Cup qualifier.
Scorers (for Italy): Antognoni, Bettega.
England: Clemence; Clement, Hughes, McFarland, Mills; Cherry, Greenhoff, Brooking; Keegan, Channon, Bowles. Sub.: Beattie (for Clement).
Match point: 'The worst England team I've ever seen. Disorganized, confused, of only modest ability and, what really let us loose, not prepared to fight back when a goal down' – Giacinto Facchetti, captain of Italy.

England 0, Holland 2: 9 February 1977.
At Wembley: 90,260.
Scorer (for Holland): Peters 2.
England: Clemence; Clement, Watson, Doyle, Beattie; Greenhoff, Madeley, Brooking; Bowles, Keegan, T. Francis. Subs.: Todd (for Greenhoff), Pearson (for Madeley).
Match points: Outclassed as badly as in the historic 6–3 victory by Hungary at Wembley in 1953. Both goals by Jan Peters, playing in only his second full match for Holland.

England 5, Luxembourg 0: 30 March 1977.
At Wembley: 81,000. World Cup qualifier.
Scorers: Keegan, T. Francis, Kennedy, Channon 2 (1 pen.).
England: Clemence; Gidman, Watson, Hughes, Cherry; Keegan, Kennedy; T. Francis, Channon, Royle, Hill. Sub.: Mariner (for Royle).
Match point: Gilbert Dresch of Luxembourg sent off in the eighty-fifth minute – only the second instance in an international match at Wembley.

England 2, Northern Ireland 1: 28 May 1977.
At Windsor Park, Belfast: 35,000.
Scorers: Channon, Tueart. Ireland: McGrath.
England: Shilton; Cherry, Todd, Watson, Mills; Wilkins, Greenhoff, Brooking; Channon, Mariner, Tueart. Sub.: Talbot (for Wilkins).
Match point: Dennis Tueart's stooping header to Brian Talbot's cross won it for England in the eighty-seventh minute, after being shocked by an Irish fifth-minute goal.

England 0, Wales 1: 31 May 1977.
At Wembley: 48,000.
Scorer (for Wales): James (pen.).
England: Shilton; Neal, Watson, Hughes, Mills; Greenhoff, Brooking, Kennedy; Keegan, Pearson, Channon. Sub.: Tueart (for Brooking).
Match point: Peter Shilton's foul on Leighton James, after a mistake by Emlyn Hughes, cost the penalty that gave Wales their first victory in England for forty-two years, and their first ever at Wembley.

England 1, Scotland 2: 4 June 1977.
At Wembley: 100,000.
Scorers: Channon (pen.). Scotland: McQueen, Dalglish.
England: Clemence; Neal, Watson, Hughes, Mills; Greenhoff, Talbot, Kennedy; T. Francis, Channon, Pearson. Subs.: Cherry (for Greenhoff), Tueart (for Kennedy).
Match point: For the first time, England had lost consecutive matches at Wembley.

England 0, Brazil 0: 8 June 1977.
At Rio: 77,000.
England: Clemence; Neal, Watson, Hughes,
Cherry; Wilkins, Talbot, Greenhoff, Keegan;
T. Francis, Pearson. Subs.: Channon (for
Pearson), Kennedy (for Wilkins).
Match point: England missed three early chances
and were then outplayed in the second half –
but saved by Ray Clemence and three on-the-
line stops by Trevor Cherry.

England 1, Argentina 1: 12 June 1977.
At Boca, Buenos Aires: 60,000.
Scorers: Pearson. Argentina: Bertoni.
England: Clemence; Neal, Watson, Hughes,
Cherry; Wilkins, Greenhoff, Talbot; Keegan,
Channon, Pearson. Sub.: Kennedy (for
Greenhoff).
Match point: Trevor Cherry, with two teeth
knocked out by a punch, was sent off with
Bertoni, whose bent free kick saved Argentina
from defeat.

England 0, Uruguay 0: 15 June 1977.
At Montevideo: 50,000.
England: Clemence; Neal, Watson, Hughes,
Cherry; Wilkins, Greenhoff, Talbot; Keegan,
Channon, Pearson.
Match point: Don Revie's final match, and one of
the dreariest ever by England. They were tired,
Uruguay were defensive.

Ron Greenwood, general manager of West Ham
United, was appointed as caretaker manager for the
last three matches of 1977. His appointment was
confirmed as full-time before the friendly against
West Germany in Munich.

England 0, Switzerland 0: 7 September 1977.
At Wembley: 42,000.
England: Clemence; Neal, Watson, Hughes,
Cherry; McDermott, Callaghan, Kennedy,
Channon, Keegan, T. Francis. Subs.: Hill (for
Channon), Wilkins (for Callaghan).
Match point: Six Liverpool players in the side –
Ray Clemence, Phil Neal, Emlyn Hughes,
Terry McDermott, Ray Kennedy and Ian
Callaghan, whose last previous appearance was
in 1966.

England 2, Luxembourg 0: 12 October 1977.
At Luxembourg: 15,000. World Cup qualifier.
Scorers: Kennedy, Mariner.
England: Clemence; Cherry, Watson, Hughes;
Callaghan, McDermott, Wilkins, Kennedy;
Hill, T. Francis, Mariner. Subs.: Whymark
(for McDermott), Beattie (for Watson).
Match point: Over-anxious, but still the first win
for seven matches.

England 2, Italy 0: 16 November 1977.
At Wembley: 92,500. World Cup qualifier.
Scorers: Keegan, Brooking.
England: Clemence; Neal, Watson, Hughes,
Cherry; Coppell, Wilkins, Brooking; Keegan,
Latchford, Barnes. Subs.: Pearson (for
Latchford), T. Francis (for Keegan).
Match point: England, with Kevin Keegan
starring, were cheered off even though the
scoreline left Italy needing only a one-goal win
against Luxembourg to qualify for Argentina.
(They won 3-0.)

England 1, West Germany 2: 22 February 1978.
At Munich: 77,850.
Scorers: Pearson. W. Germany: Worm, Bonhof.
England: Clemence; Neal, Watson, Hughes,
Mills; Coppell, Wilkins, Brooking; Keegan,
Pearson, Barnes. Sub.: T. Francis (for
Keegan).
Match point: German substitute Ronnie Worm's
second-half equalizer made him the first player
ever to score against England on successive
nights – for the previous evening he had scored
a goal against the 'B' team in Augsburg.

England 1, Brazil 1: 19 April 1978.
At Wembley: 92,500.
Scorers: Keegan. Brazil: Gil.
England: Corrigan; Mills, Watson, Greenhoff,
Cherry; Keegan, Currie; Coppell, T. Francis,
Latchford, Barnes.
Match point: Brazil, a goal up after ten minutes,
obstructed and chopped and had five players
booked. England equalized from a free kick.

England 3, Wales 1: 13 May 1978.
At Cardiff: 17,698.

Scorers: Latchford, Currie, Barnes. Wales:
  Dwyer.
England: Shilton; Mills, Watson, Greenhoff,
  Cherry; Wilkins, Brooking; Coppell,
  T. Francis, Latchford, Barnes. Subs.: Currie
  (for Cherry), Mariner (for Latchford).
Match point: Trevor Cherry broke a shoulder in
  the first half, so Ray Wilkins switched to full
  back – but England won with late goals,
  featuring a 35-yarder by Tony Currie.

England 1, Northern Ireland 0: 16 May 1978.
At Wembley: 50,000.
Scorer: Neal.
England: Clemence; Neal, Watson, Hughes,
  Mills; Currie, Wilkins, Greenhoff; Coppell,
  Pearson, Woodcock.
Match point: Irish goalkeeper Jim Platt stars.

England 1, Scotland 0: 20 May 1978.
At Hampden Park: 88,319.
Scorer: Coppell.
England: Clemence; Neal, Watson, Hughes,
  Mills; Currie, Wilkins; Coppell, Francis,
  Mariner, Barnes. Subs.: Greenhoff (for
  Hughes), Brooking (for Mariner).
Match point: Dave Watson outstanding in an
  England side generally outplayed – yet they
  regained the championship when goalkeeper
  Alan Rough dropped a cross from Peter Barnes.

England 4, Hungary 1: 24 May 1978.
At Wembley: 74,000.
Scorers: Barnes, Neal (pen.), T. Francis, Currie.
  Hungary: Nagy.
England: Shilton; Neal, Watson, Hughes, Mills;
  Wilkins, Brooking; Coppell, T. Francis,
  Keegan, Barnes. Subs.: Greenhoff (for
  Watson), Currie (for Coppell).
Match point: England, with no orthodox centre
  forward, gained a 3-0 lead in the first forty
  minutes. The star: Kevin Keegan.

England 4, Denmark 3: 20 September 1978.
At Copenhagen: 47,600. European championship
  qualifier.
Scorers: Keegan 2, Latchford, Neal. Denmark:
  Simonsen (pen.), Arnesen, Rontved.

England: Clemence; Neal, Watson, Hughes,
  Mills; Wilkins, Brooking; Coppell, Latchford,
  Keegan, Barnes.
Match point: Kevin Keegan headed two goals
  from free kicks but the lead was lost within five
  minutes. England regained it but then let the
  Danes score again. 'I'm an advocate of
  attacking football, but this carried it to
  extremes,' said Ron Greenwood.

England 1, Irish Republic 1: 25 October 1978.
At Dublin: 50,000. European championship
  qualifier.
Scorers: Latchford. Irish: Daly.
England: Clemence; Neal, Watson, Hughes,
  Mills; Wilkins, Brooking; Coppell, Latchford,
  Keegan, Barnes. Subs.: Thompson (for
  Watson), Woodcock (for Barnes).
Match points: England opened briskly and scored
  with a header, but were disorganized by an
  early injury to Dave Watson. Star: Steve
  Coppell.

England 1, Czechoslovakia 0: 29 November 1978.
At Wembley: 92,000.
Scorer: Coppell.
England: Shilton; Anderson, Thompson,
  Watson, Cherry; Wilkins, Currie; Coppell,
  Keegan, Woodcock, Barnes. Sub.: Latchford
  (for Woodcock).
Match points: Viv Anderson became the first
  black England international. Ron Greenwood
  said: 'Spoiled by a frozen pitch. The Czechs
  were better balanced and controlled, but we
  battled for a result.' Star: Peter Shilton.

England 4, Northern Ireland 0: 7 February 1979.
At Wembley: 92,000. European championship
  qualifier.
Scorers: Keegan, Latchford 2, Watson.
England: Clemence; Neal, Watson, Hughes,
  Mills; Coppell, Currie, Brooking; Latchford,
  Keegan, Barnes.
Match point: Kevin Keegan at his best. He
  headed a brave first goal, crossed to Bob
  Latchford for the second, and back-headed
  Trevor Brooking's short corner to make the
  fourth.

Northern Ireland 0, England 2: 19 May 1979.
At Belfast: 35,000.
Scorers: Watson, Coppell.
England: Clemence; Neal, Thompson, Watson,
Mills; McDermott, Wilkins, Currie; Coppell,
Latchford, Barnes.
Match point: Two goals in the first 16 minutes
finished it as a contest.

England 0, Wales 0: 23 May 1979.
At Wembley: 70,220.
England: Corrigan; Cherry, Watson, Hughes,
Sansom; McDermott, Currie, Wilkins;
Cunningham, Keegan, Latchford. Subs:
Coppell (for Latchford), Brooking (for Currie).
Match point: 'Our finishing was bad' – Ron
Greenwood.

England 3, Scotland 1: 26 May 1979.
At Wembley: 100,000.
Scorers: Barnes, Coppell, Keegan. Scotland:
Wark.
England: Clemence; Neal, Thompson, Watson,
Mills; Coppell, Wilkins, Brooking; Barnes,
Keegan, Latchford.
Match point: England retain the home champion-
ship after a victory stemming from a mistake by
keeper George Wood when Steve Coppell
scored.

Bulgaria 0, England 3: 6 June 1979.
At Sofia: 55,000. European Championship.
Scorers: Keegan, Watson, Barnes.
England: Clemence; Neal, Thompson, Watson,
Mills; Coppell, Wilkins, Brooking; Latchford,
Keegan, Barnes. Subs: Francis (for Latchford),
Woodcock (for Barnes).
Match point: Headers by Dave Watson and Peter
Barnes in the 54th and 55th minutes killed off
Bulgaria. 'A superb team performance in
difficult heat,' said Ron Greenwood.

Sweden 0, England 0: 10 June 1979.
At Stockholm: 35,356.
England: Shilton; Anderson, Hughes, Watson,
Cherry; McDermott, Keegan, Currie; Francis,
Woodcock, Cunningham. Subs: Thompson
(for Watson), Wilkins (for McDermott),
Brooking (for Currie).

Match point: Emlyn Hughes, hitting the crossbar
after a 60-yard run in the first-half, came
nearest to scoring.

Austria 4, England 3: 13 June 1979.
At Vienna: 31,000.
Scorers: Keegan, Coppell, Wilkins. Austria:
Pezzey 2, Welzl 2.
England: Shilton; Neal, Thompson, Watson,
Mills; Wilkins, Brooking; Coppell, Keegan,
Latchford, Barnes. Subs: Clemence (for
Shilton), Francis (for Latchford), Cunningham
(for Barnes).
Match point: England, 3-1 down at half time,
fought back to 3-3 but lost to Pezzey's header
at a free kick.

Index

Page numbers in italics refer to illustrations.

Allison, Malcolm, 74
America, *see* United States tournament
Antonio, George, 75
Ardiles, Osvaldo, 40
Argentina (*see also* World Cup, 1978),
33-4, 61-3, *62, 63*
Aston, Johnny, 47
'attacking teams', 56
attitudes, national: Brazilian, 39;
Dutch, 36-7; East German, 34;
English, 28; Russian, 34; Scottish,
28; Welsh, 27; West German, 37-9;
Yugoslav, 37
autographs, 100, *111*
Ayala, Hugo, 33

Baily, Ken (England mascot), *106,
107,* 108-9
Ball, Alan, 11-12, 17, 23, 52, 97;
Revie dismisses him, 23
Banks, Gordon, 77, 128, *128*
Barnes, Peter, 69, *81*
Beattie, Kevin, 52, 97
Beckenbauer, Franz, 124-6, *125*;
compared with Moore, 124
Belfast, 30, 64
Belgrade, incident with airport guards,
49, *49*
Bell, Colin, 12-13, 30, 31, 57, *147*
Benetti, Romeo, 19, 86, 126
Best, George, 131, *131*
Bettega, Roberto, *124*
Boca Juniors stadium, 61-3, *62, 87*
Bonhof, Rainer, 19, 92, 118, 119, *120*
Bowles, Stan, 55, 85, 101
boxing, 113
Brady, Liam, 116, 137
Brandts, Erny, 34
Brazil, 39, 69, 94
Brazilian attitudes, 39
Bremner, Billy, 50, 130, *130*
British XI, Keegan's selection, 128-31
Broderick, Cyril 'Brod', 72
Brooking, Trevor 'Hadleigh', *18-19,*
55, 79, 83, 103, *103*
Buenos Aires, 61-3
Burrows, Dr Peter, 71-2
Busby, Sir Matt, 11, 71

Capello, Fabio, *83*

caps, international, 11
captaincy, England, 10-11; leadership,
69
Cerezo, 32
Channon, Mick, 28, 49, 53, 56, 57, 60,
101, 108; captain in U.S. tournament
match, 60; gambling, 101; Keegan's
favourite footballer, 100; playing
style, 55; and Revie's dossiers, 53
Charlton, Bobby, 11, 17, 13, 110, 130,
130
Cherry, Trevor, 54, 55, 61, 63
Chivers, Martin, 12, 22
Clarke, Allan, 58
Clemence, Ray, 31, 61, 63, 118, 119;
Peter Shilton, 77-80; professional
foul, 56
Clement, Dave, 54
Clough, Brian, 43, 43-6, 45, 46, 71,
102
coaches and coaching, 69-71, 72;
English and German, 74, 121
Cocker, Les, 61, 70, 71, 74
Cohen, George, 129-30
Coppell, Steve, 68, 69, 93, 137, 138,
139
Cormack, Peter, 29
Coutinho, Claudio, 39, 40
Croker, Ted, 71
Cruyff, Johan, 33, 36, 37, 57, 95,
126-8, 127
Cuccureddu, Antonello, 54
Cullis, Stan, 25
Cunningham, Laurie, 9
Currie, Tony, 69, 119
Cyprus, 30, 102
Czechoslovakia, 57, 57-8, 58, 93, 139

Dalglish, Kenny, 31, 78
Daly, Gerry, 137, 138
death threat to Keegan, 30
Denmark, 94, 137
Dewis, George, 77
Deyna, Kasiu, 40, 41
Disneyland, 84
Dobson, Martin, 21
dossiers, Revie's, 53-4
Dublin, 137
Dutch attitudes, 36-7

East German attitudes, 34
East Germany, 11, 34
Edwards, Duncan, 73
Eire, *see* Irish Republic
Enckelman, Goran, 55
England, Mike, 60
English arrogance, 28
English game, attitudes to: Brazilian,
39; German, 41; Italian, 39-40

English players abroad, 134

Facchetti, Giacinto, *89*, 123–4
fan club, Keegan's, 111
fans, 107–11; Scottish, 29, *29*
Finland, 55, *55*, *56*
Finney, Tom, *47*
forwards, *13*, 55
fouls, 25, *32*, 35, 39–40, 63, 116–17;
    professional, 56
Fox, Norman, 60
Francis, Gerry, 30, 57, 97
Francis, Trevor, 9, 27, *27*, 44, *45*, 102,
    102
Franklin, Neil, *47*
free kicks, 119
Froggatt, Jack, *47*

Gallego, Amenico, *155*
gambling, 101
Germany, East, 11, 34
Germany, West, 113–19; house buy-
    ing, 113, *115*; language problems,
    113, 115–16; suspensions, 117;
    team-talks, 116; training, 74;
    transfer fee, 116; view of English
    goalkeepers, 80
Giles, Johnny, 137
Gillard, Ian, 58
Gillies, Matt, 74
goalkeepers, 77–80; Continental view
    of English, 78–80
Gordon, Jimmy, *46*
Gorgon, Jerzy, 124, *125*
Greaves, Jimmy, *43*
Greenhoff, Brian, 55
Greenwood, Ron, 10, *43*, 65, 67, *68*;
    apprentice signwriter, 65, 66; and
    co-operation between clubs and
    England, 133–4; and free kicks, 119;
    players' freedom under him, 66;
    receptiveness to ideas, 66–7, 121;
    recruitment of managers and
    coaches, 69–70; sayings, 66, 137
Gujdar, Sandor, *86*

Haan, Arie, *38*
Hamburg, *112*, 113–17, 119; release
    for international games, 134
'hard-man' football, 20
Heighway, Steve, *26*, 43, 103–5, *105*
Hill, Gordon, 100
Hockey, Trevor, 27
Holland, 36–7, *37*, 56–7
Holmes, Nick, 150
Holzenbein, Bernd, *118*
home internationals, 25–31; lack of
    atmosphere, 25; numbers of Scots
    at, 29; 'treason factor', 27
Howe, Don, *43*, 71, 72, 74
Hudson, Alan, 22, *22*
Hughes, Emlyn, 67–9, 97, 100
Hurst, Geoff, *47*, 64, 70, 74–5, 130–1

insults, 109–11
international games, players' release
    for, 133–4
invalid cars, 134–5
Ireland, Northern, 30, 138
Irish Republic, 31, 137, *156*
Iron Curtain countries, 11, 34–6

Jairzinho, *145*
James, Leighton, 31
Jennings, Pat, *26*, 90, *136*, 137
John, Elton, 107–8, *108*
Johnson, David, *33*
Johnstone, Jimmy, 130, *130*, *131*
Jones, Joey, 25
Jongbloed, Jan, *38*

Keegan, Jean, 30, 100, 114, *114*, 115,
    117
Keegan, Laura-Jane, *132*, 134
keepers, *see* goalkeepers
Kempes, Mario, *33*, 33–4, 126, 128
Kennedy, Ray, *15*
Kenyon, Roger, 52
Krohn, Dr Peter, *111*, 116

Landsdowne Road rugby ground, 138

Latchford, Bob, 98, 137, *142*
leadership of captain, 69
Leao, Emerson, 59
Leeds, 51, 52
Lindsay, Alec, 20
Lisbon, 58
Liverpool, 51, 52
London players, northerners' attitude
    to, 103
Lorimer, Peter, 43–4
Luque, Leo, 38

Macdonald, Malcolm 'Supermac', 98,
    100, 101
McGrain, Danny, *31*, 129, *129*
McMenemy, Lawrie, 21
McQueen, Gordon, 29
Maier, Sepp, 59, 118, 123, *124*, *149*
managers (*see also individual names*),
    43–9; and players' freedom of
    speech, 44
Mancini, Terry 'Henry', *104*, 105
Maracana stadium, 60, 61
Marsh, Rodney, 12
mascot, England (Ken Baily), *106*,
    107, 108–9
Masny, Marian, *57*
Mears, Brian, 71, *71*
Medhurst, Norman, 72
Mercer, Joe, 20, *21*, 43, 48, 48–9
Millichip, Bert, 71
Mills, Mick, 69, 118, 119, 138
modelling, Keegan's, *134*
money incentives, 51, 61
Moore, Bobby, 14–15, *15*, 28; as
    captain, 69, 97, *98*; as choice for
    Keegan's British XI, 130; compared
    with Beckenbauer, 124; hundredth
    cap, 28; Keegan's first game against,
    14–15; with Team America, 59, *59*,
    61
Morgan, Willie, 29
Muhren, Arnold, 41
Mullen, Gerd 'Der Bomber', *38*, 39,
    126, 128
Mulligan, Paddy, *156*
Munich, *38*, 90, 92, 118, *118*, *149*
Munro, Frank, *31*

national characteristics, *see* attitudes,
    national
Neal, Phil, 138
Neeskens, Johan, 36, *37*, 57, *88*, 123
Nelson, Sammy, *136*
Netzer, Gunter, 20
northerners' attitudes to London
    players, 103
Northern Ireland, 30, *90*, 138, *139*

Odell, Alan, 71
O'Leary, David, 137

Pearson, Stan, *47*
Pearson, Stuart, 118
Pele, 59, 60, *122*, 126, *127*, 128, *145*
Passarella, Daniel, *87*, *155*
Perryman, Steve, 21
Phillips, John, 83
Phillips, Dr Neil, 49
Poland, 9, *147*
poltergeist in America, 60
positions in team, 31, 55
pressure games, 61
Preuss, Erhard, 113, 116–17

Ramsey, Sir Alf, 9, 11, *42*, 43, 47; as
    England manager, 46–8; 'one man
    band', 71; on players' release for
    international matches, 133; supports
    Keegan in Under-23 matches, 11
Rattin, Antonio, 61
referees, 63, 131
Regis, Cyrille, 9
Rep, Johnny, 36, *37*, *155*
Rest of the World fixtures, 123
Revie, Don, 10, 29, 43, 50, 51–63, *52*,
    70, 71, *100*; bingo and putting
    sessions, 52; builds characterless
    squad, 21–3; dossiers, 53–4; faults,
    53; and free kicks, 119; Keegan
    walks out on him, 10, 30; and press,

53; selection errors, 55–6; signs for
    United Arab Emirates, 63; team
    song, 52, 59; team-talks, 51–2
Rimmer, Jimmy, *104*
Rio de Janeiro, 60, 61
Rivelino, Roberto, 126, *126*
Roberts, John, 24
Robson, Bobby, 71, 72, *73*
Rodrigues, Rui, 58
Rome 1980, 137
rooms, sharing, 98–9
Rowley, Jack, *47*
Royle, Joe, 56
rugby pitches, 138
Russians, 34, *36*

Schoen, Helmut, 118
Schrecker, Robert, 107, *108*, 109, *109*
Scots: attitudes, 28; fans, 29, *29*
Seeler, Uwe, 75
Sexton, Dave, 71, 72
Shankly, Bill, 13–15, *14*, 77, 123, 139
Shilton, Peter, 74, *76*, 77–80, *78*, *79*,
    119
Smith, Tommy, *14*, 60, 126
song, England team, 52, 59
Spence, Derek, 27
Sprake, Gary, 12, *13*
Stiles, Nobby, 19, *42*
Storey, Peter, 19–20
Street, Fred, *52*, 72
Streten, Bernard, *47*
Suurbier, Wim, 36
Swales, Peter, 71

Tardelli, Marco, 19
Taylor, Bill, 71, 74, 99
Taylor, Jack, 131
Taylor, Peter, 21, 31, *45*, *46*, 71
Team America, 59, *59*
Thomas, Dave, 21
Thompson, Professor Sir Harold, 71
Todd, Colin, 97
Tomaszewski, Jan, *8*, 9, *147*
training: in England, 35, 50, 52, 67,
    68, 74; in Germany, 74, *117*, 121

Tueart, Dennis, 56

Under-23 matches, 11
United Arab Emirates, 63
United States tournament, 58–61, *59*

van der Kerkhof, Willy, *33*, 34
Venables, Terry, 70, 71, 72–4
Vogts, Berti, *116*, 124, *124*

Wales, 24; centenary match, 31;
    nationalist fervour, 27
walls, 119
warm-ups, 41
Watson, Dave, *39*, *83*, 97–8, 130, 138
Watson, Willie, *47*
Welsh attitudes, 27
Welsh crowds, 29
Wembley: defects of, 19; Keegan's
    debut, 12
West German attitudes, 37–9
West Germany, *see* Germany, West
Wilkins, Ray, 69, 102–3, *121*
Williams, Bert, *47*
Wilson, Ray, 129–30, *129*
Winterbottom, Sir Walter, 43, *43*
Wiseman, Jack, 71
Woodcock, Bruce, 113
Woodcock, Tony, 9
work-rate, 30, *91*; Revie's appreciation
    of, 30
World XI, Keegan's selection, 123–8
World Cup: 1966, 11, *47*, 129; 1970,
    15, 17, *127*, 130, *145*; 1974, *37*, 38;
    1978, *33*, 34, 38, 39, 81, 94, 101,
    102, 104; 1982, 139
Worm, Ronnie, 118
Worthington, Frank, 102, *104*
Wragg, Dick, 71
Wright, Billy, *47*

Yugoslavs, 37

Zebec, Branco, *117*, 121, 123
Zoff, Dino, 10, 54, 55, 67–9, 96, 123

Photo acknowledgements

The author and publisher would like to thank the following for supplying and/or giving permission to reproduce the illustrations on the pages listed: All Sport, page 95 (Tony Duffy); Associated Press, 119; Owen Barnes, 90 bottom, 93; Camera Press, 60 (G/S), 106 (Roger Crump), 115 (Sven Simon), 122 (Jungkwan Chi), 128 (Colour Sports/RBO), 140 (G/M); Colorsport, 1, 16, 20, 67, 68 bottom, 81, 83 top, 84, 86 (2), 88, 89, 90 top, 91, 92, 94 top, 96, 112, 138 left, 142; *Daily Mirror*, 65 (Monte Fresco); Keystone, 6, 8, 28, 29, 37 (2), 38 bottom, 39, 42, 43, 47 top, 52, 54 (2), 55, 57 left, 63, 70 bottom left, 73, 99 bottom, 125 bottom, 127 bottom, 147, 149, 153, 156; Popperfoto, 111 bottom, 134; Robert Schrecker, 108 right, 109; Sporting Pictures (U.K.) Ltd, 82, 94 bottom, 116, 118, 120, 121; Syndication International, 2–3, 10, 11, 13, 14, 15, 18–19, 21, 22, 23, 24, 26, 27, 31, 32, 33, 34, 35, 36, 38 top, 40 (3), 45 (2), 46, 47 bottom, 48, 49, 50, 53, 56, 57 right, 58, 59, 62, 64, 68 top, 70 top and bottom right, 71, 76, 78, 79 (2), 80, 83 bottom, 85, 87, 98, 99 top, 100, 101, 102, 103, 104, 105, 108 left, 110, 111 top, 114 (2), 117, 124 (2), 125 top, 126, 127 top, 129 (2), 130 (2), 131, 132, 133, 135, 136, 138 right, 139 (2), 145, 150, 155.

Northern Ireland 0, England 2: 19 May 1979.
At Belfast: 35,000.
Scorers: Watson, Coppell.
England: Clemence; Neal, Thompson, Watson, Mills; McDermott, Wilkins, Currie; Coppell, Latchford, Barnes.
Match point: Two goals in the first 16 minutes finished it as a contest.

England 0, Wales 0: 23 May 1979.
At Wembley: 70,220.
England: Corrigan; Cherry, Watson, Hughes, Sansom; McDermott, Currie, Wilkins; Cunningham, Keegan, Latchford. Subs: Coppell (for Latchford), Brooking (for Currie).
Match point: 'Our finishing was bad' – Ron Greenwood.

England 3, Scotland 1: 26 May 1979.
At Wembley: 100,000.
Scorers: Barnes, Coppell, Keegan. Scotland: Wark.
England: Clemence; Neal, Thompson, Watson, Mills; Coppell, Wilkins, Brooking; Barnes, Keegan, Latchford.
Match point: England retain the home championship after a victory stemming from a mistake by keeper George Wood when Steve Coppell scored.

Bulgaria 0, England 3: 6 June 1979.
At Sofia: 55,000. European Championship.
Scorers: Keegan, Watson, Barnes.
England: Clemence; Neal, Thompson, Watson, Mills; Coppell, Wilkins, Brooking; Latchford, Keegan, Barnes. Subs: Francis (for Latchford), Woodcock (for Barnes).
Match point: Headers by Dave Watson and Peter Barnes in the 54th and 55th minutes killed off Bulgaria. 'A superb team performance in difficult heat,' said Ron Greenwood.

Sweden 0, England 0: 10 June 1979.
At Stockholm: 35,356.
England: Shilton; Anderson, Hughes, Watson, Cherry; McDermott, Keegan, Currie; Francis, Woodcock, Cunningham. Subs: Thompson (for Watson), Wilkins (for McDermott), Brooking (for Currie).

Match point: Emlyn Hughes, hitting the crossbar after a 60-yard run in the first-half, came nearest to scoring.

Austria 4, England 3: 13 June 1979.
At Vienna: 31,000.
Scorers: Keegan, Coppell, Wilkins. Austria: Pezzey 2, Welzl 2.
England: Shilton; Neal, Thompson, Watson, Mills; Wilkins, Brooking; Coppell, Keegan, Latchford, Barnes. Subs: Clemence (for Shilton), Francis (for Latchford), Cunningham (for Barnes).
Match point: England, 3-1 down at half time, fought back to 3-3 but lost to Pezzey's header at a free kick.

Index

Page numbers in italics refer to illustrations.

Allison, Malcolm, 74
America, *see* United States tournament
Antonio, George, 75
Ardiles, Osvaldo, *40*
Argentina (*see also* World Cup, 1978), 33-4, 61-3, *62, 63*
Aston, Johnny, *47*
'attacking teams', 56
attitudes, national: Brazilian, 39; Dutch, 36-7; East German, 34; English, 28; Russian, 34; Scottish, 28; Welsh, 27; West German, 37-9; Yugoslav, 37
autographs, 100, *111*
Ayala, Hugo, 33

Baily, Ken (England mascot), *106, 107*, 108-9
Ball, Alan, 11-12, 17, *23, 52*, 97; Revie dismisses him, 23
Banks, Gordon, 77, 128, *128*
Barnes, Peter, 69, *81*
Beattie, Kevin, *52*, 97
Beckenbauer, Franz, 124-6, *125*; compared with Moore, 124
Belfast, 30, *64*
Belgrade, incident with airport guards, 49, *49*
Bell, Colin, 12-13, 30, 31, 57, *147*
Benetti, Romeo, 19, *86*, 126
Best, George, 131, *131*
Bettega, Roberto, *124*
Boca Juniors stadium, 61-3, *62*, 87
Bonhof, Rainer, 19, *92*, 118, 119, *120*
Bowles, Stan, 55, *85*, 101
boxing, 113
Brady, Liam, 116, 137
Brandts, Erny, *34*
Brazil, 39, 69, *94*
Brazilian attitudes, 39
Bremner, Billy, 50, 130, *130*
British XI, Keegan's selection, 128-31
Broderick, Cyril 'Brod', *72*
Brooding, Trevor 'Hadleigh', *18-19*, 55, 79, *83*, 103, *103*
Buenos Aires, 61 3
Burrows, Dr Peter, 71-2
Busby, Sir Matt, *11*, 71

Capello, Fabio, *83*

caps, international, 11
captaincy, England, 10-11; leadership, 69
Cerezo, *32*
Channon, Mick, *28, 49, 53, 56, 57, 60, 101*, 108; captain in U.S. tournament match, 60; gambling, 101; Keegan's favourite footballer, 100; playing style, 55; and Revie's dossiers, 53
Charlton, Bobby, *11*, 17, *43, 110*, 130, *130*
Cherry, Trevor, *54, 55*, 61, 63
Chivers, Martin, 12, 22
Clarke, Allan, *58*
Clemence, Ray, 31, 61, 63, 118, 119; Peter Shilton, 77-80; professional foul, 56
Clement, Dave, *54*
Clough, Brian, *43*, 43-6, *45*, 46, 71, 102
coaches and coaching, 69-71, 72; English and German, 74, 121
Cocker, Les, 61, *70*, 71, 74
Cohen, George, 129-30
Coppell, Steve, 68, 69, *93*, 137, *138, 139*
Cormack, Peter, 29
Coutinho, Claudio, 39, *40*
Croker, Ted, 71
Cruyff, Johan, 33, 36, *37*, 57, *95*, 126-8, *127*
Cuccureddu, Antonello, *54*
Cullis, Stan, 25
Cunningham, Laurie, 9
Currie, Tony, 69, 119
Cyprus, 30, 102
Czechoslovakia, *57*, 57-8, *58*, 93, *139*

Dalglish, Kenny, 31, 78
Daly, Gerry, 137, *138*
death threat to Keegan, 30
Denmark, *94*, 137
Dewis, George, *11*
Deyna, Kasiu, *40*, 41
Disneyland, *84*
Dobson, Martin, 21
dossiers, Revie's, 53-4
Dublin, 137
Dutch attitudes, 36-7

East German attitudes, 34
East Germany, 11, 34
Edwards, Duncan, *73*
Eire, *see* Irish Republic
Enckelman, Goran, *55*
England, Mike, 60
English arrogance, 28
English game, attitudes to: Brazilian, 39; German, 41; Italian, 39-40